HACKING THE FUTURE

STORIES FOR THE FLESH-EATING 90S

CultureTexts

Arthur and Marilouise Kroker   General Editors

CultureTexts is a series of creative explorations of the theory, politics and culture of hypermodern society.

Titles

HACKING THE FUTURE

STORIES FOR THE FLESH-EATING 90S

ARTHUR & MARILOUISE KROKER

ST. MARTIN'S PRESS
NEW YORK

HACKING THE FUTURE

© 1996 by New World Perspectives
CultureTexts Series

St. Martin's Press, Scholarly and Reference Division,
175 Fifth Avenue, New York, N.Y. 10010

First published in the United States of America in 1996

Printed in Canada

ISBN 0-312-12955-6

Arthur Kroker's contribution to *Hacking the Future* was facilitated by a research grant
from the Social Sciences and Humanities Research Council of Canada.

Library of Congress Cataloging-in-Publication Data

Kroker, Arthur, 1945-
    Hacking the future : stories for the flesh-eating 90s / Arthur &
Marilouise Kroker.
      p. cm. -- (CultureTexts)
    Includes bibliographical references and index.
    ISBN 0-312-12955-6 (pbk.)
    1. Technology and civilization.   2. Computers and civilization.
3. Civilization. Modern--1950-   4. Culture.   I. Kroker, Marilouise.
II. Title.   III. Series.
HM211.K737   1995
303.483--dc20   95-25802
                                                      CIP

Hacking the Future

THE AMERICAN ALGORITHM

Slash and Burn
Branded Flesh
"Brains Live a Little Bit Longer"

C O D E   W A R R I O R S

Slumming in Gopher Space
Las Vegas Trilogy
  From Silicon Illusions to Desert Dreamlands
  Treasure Island at the Mirage
  Las Vegas Theme Park
The Clam King
Shopping the Sky: Majorica Pearls at 5 Miles Up
Luminous Luxor Las Vegas
UFO's in Yuma, Arizona
Ebola Virus
Time for a TUMS
Hacking the Xerox Alphabet

P I N H O L I N G   T H E   M A L L

Shopping the GAP with Nietzsche
Shopping the Infomercial Highway
Shopping for Time
Victoria's Secret
Baudrillard at the Express
The Lemon Yellow Coat
Silver Lady on QVC
Talking Daytime TV

D O O R S   O F   M I S P E R C E P T I O N

H A C K I N G   T H E   F U T U R E

THE AMERICAN ALGORITHM

Going to the Country

Marilouise

It's 1968 and I'm in a car on my way from Boston to the Canadian border. Thinking "What a wonderful day for America," I check out my immigration papers for exiting the States. **Canned Heat** *are singing on the radio "We Might Even Leave the USA..."*

And I did.

Arthur

It's 1968 and I've left the seminary and I'm heading down to America. What a wonderful day for me!

Not to the East or West coasts, but to the heart of the heartland, Lafayette, Indiana, with its Kentucky sharecroppers drifting north to work piece-rate in the machine tool factories, and with its trumpet calls through the night for all the Hoosiers of the world to fess up to their Indiana birthright, and with all the madness and sadness and boredom and delirium that was Lafayette on my mind. I was in the dead heart of America, and I had a lot to learn.

Four years later, sick of heart at the War and the assassinations and with intimations of violent times of reckoning to come, I'm packing my Mustang for the trip back to Canada to think about it all again. Someone slaps a bumper sticker on my rear fender: "America: Love it or Leave it."

And I did.

NO IMMUNITY

Most societies desperately try to immunize themselves against the blast of digital technology. The European Community freeze-dries culture in museums, sometimes transforming whole cities into walking, talking theme parks. The Canadian Government specializes in creating circuit-breakers (regulatory structures) to stop the flow of digital technology. Telephones, banks, and insurance companies: that's the Canadian beaver pond, and like all tranquil pools, the point is to stop the flow of escaping water. Which is strange because Canadians themselves are digital beings: born with modems in their pockets, chips for heads, pixels for eyes, with satellites on their minds, 3D accelerators on their feet for speed travel across the multi-graphical interfaces of the Net in their flesh, WEB personalities, and deep space radio telemetry as nervous systems. Being digital is being Canadian because Canadians see themselves as improved Americans.

Improved Americans? Americans are different. They actually tear down immunity defenses in order to feel the raw pleasure that comes from the hit of the digital dynamo when it puts its hooks into human flesh. McLuhan was thinking of Americans when he said: "How are you to argue with people who insist on sticking their heads in the invisible teeth of technology, calling the whole thing freedom?" But, then again, what else are you going to do if you want to be razor sharp?

From the outside looking in, America seems deceptively simple. Aliens wonder how this nation of jocks, Christian barbecue suburbanites, and Hollywood actor politicians, and rappers and rockers and drug dealers and armed-to-the-assault-rifle teeth wilderness fundamentalists, not only got a world empire, but actually managed to keep it. With a mixture of contempt and envy, the world gazes into the looking-glass of America and sees only a clown's face toting a Saturday Night Special. Condescendingly they declare: "We see with clearer eyes and better brains and, after all, we have history on our side. *We* should be America."

A restless nation of transients who cut their Oedipal ties to Europe with a political revolution, America began with no history before the age of progress. "No Immunity" is the battlecry of a people who like their identity strong. Every American louder than life summer tourist strolling on a foreign beach can seem so relaxed on the surface because the internal codes are coiled so tight and learned so well at such an early age.

Shucking off talk of a social contract or a divine right of kings and spitting on the noblesse oblige of "civilizational discourse," American identity is technology. And we don't mean technology as prosthetics or technology as a servomechanism of the struggling inner self, but two-fingered tech, make that straight up and no ice please. Like a chip factory running flat out, the American self plops off the electronic conveyor-belt with wired flesh.

The age of science might have slowly come to maturity in Europe, beating its head against the drag-me-down fetters of feudal aristocracy and deeply ingrained religious prejudice, but in America science gets a green card, and is waved right past Ellis Island on a fast pass to everywhere. Here, all the insurrectionary codes of the scientific method — reification of nature, objectification of the body, radical experimentalism of thought, of action, of desire — just slip out of the dry pages of the philosophical tomes and flesh-net themselves into that quantum marvel of the New World: the American self. Nobody can teach Americans anything about the real lessons of science and technology. Scratch an American and you'll find a relativity theorist, a brilliant textbook example in the guise of a stockbroker, suburbanite, or New Age rural retreatist of a living, breathing dynamic field-event. Margaret Atwood must have been thinking of Americans when she said: "I'm a site where action happens." No wonder Americans look so relaxed. Like brownian motion, they can bubble away on the effervescent surface because the reaction-formations lie deep and lie strong in the test-tube of the American self. Or, as one American software designer responded when asked whether or not it was true that the United States had committed itself fully to the will to technology: "Sounds right, I guess we're just wired that way."

Tech flesh: that's the secret of the American algorithm.

PUTTING DOWN CODE IN THE USA

The American Algorithm? That's America as the Operating System for global culture at the beginning of the 3rd millennium. Some countries specialize in technological hardware, others in digital wetware: but America produces software for contemporary culture. Not just computer software — America creates the key technological codes that drive world culture, economy, and society. When the American algorithm is reprogrammed, shifting, for example, from the technological liberalism of the early Clinton Administration to the conservative fundamentalism of Gingrich's "Contract with America," then the world doesn't just sneeze, it immediately gets digitally updated with the newest generation of the American code. The techno-optimism of liberal futurism is dumped into the trash, and the world bunkers down for a lean and mean period as technoculture is reorganized around the politics of rationalization and Spencerian economics. In the American vernacular, this means that stories about digital reality now move directly from the business pages to the front page of the daily newspaper. What's on-line in the business pages is what's coded, or about to be coded, in the American mind. By the mid-90s, American business actively and overtly makes foreign policy, for example, separating trade issues from human rights, that is, torture from profit. Technobusiness likes to say that trade encourages the possibility of human rights by opening up alien societies to external contact. What they never mention is that trade also legitimizes and, in most cases, prolongs torture governments. But then, in America technology, particularly technobusiness, rules. The first software code of America is that technology is life, and, consequently, that being technology *is* the American mind.

MICROAMERICA

As the software that provides system-operating codes for global culture, America powers up the 21st century. When McLuhan said that America *is* the world environment, he is to be taken literally. Tech hardware may provide external prosthetics for the digital addiction, and tech wetware may interface the body and the Net, but software is the distributive intelligence that authors the system. Just ask IBM, whose mainframe hardware monoliths were like digital dinosaurs crashing around wired culture, supposedly impervious to challenge, just before Bill's cyber-gates opened up, releasing software raptors into the feeding chain. The rest is virtual history.

In the late 20th century, software is the power principle. And it is here that Americans have a special advantage. Unlike other countries which approach writing software as a learned technical skill, Americans take to software like a cookout and fireworks on the 4th of July. Writing software is actually like writing out in code what it means to be an American. American software genius lies in coding, decoding, and recoding. Authoring both Operating Systems- *and* Terminal Systems logic, America jams the extremes together, and pushes ahead with the difference. That *difference* is what's called "reinventing America," and "renewing America." There is a lot left behind when America spurts ahead with every turn of the (software) wheel, but that's alright. A fundamental tenet of American citizenship is that nothing should stand in the way of the will to technology. Safety nets can be provided, therapy classes can be mandated for those unable, or unwilling, to cope with rapid technological change, and anti-anxiety drugs can be distributed to the rest.

The basis of American identity is the will to technology. Only Americans have been courageous, or maniacal, enough to pay the price for the coming to be of virtual reality. They are Nietzsche's experimental subjects who transform themselves into nutcrackers of the soul, objects of conscience and body-vivisectioning. They can be observed from a distance by Asians, Europeans and Canadians with a mixture of adulation, scorn and feelings of cultural superiority, but not without a lingering sense of deep admiration and awe for these Kings and Queens of the virtual kingdom.

America is the most aestheticized country in the world. Not aesthetics in the melancholic *fin-de-siecle* sense or the modernist sense of splitting high art from popular culture, but the American Homepage as all about interfacing digital technology and popular culture to produce Web identity, tech culture, virtual economy, and recombinant politics. What late 19th century sociologists called "collective consciousness" has been transformed in virtual America into "Web consciousness." *Being Digital* means knowing your telematic place on the American Homepage, and believing, really believing, in the utopian possibility of reinventing your destiny by hypertext technology. Canadians might have the luxury of viewing communications as a work of high art, but Americans don't wear cultural blinkers: communications is war.

AMERICA'S HOMEPAGE

In America, the World Wide Web is not just a matter of hyperlinks or hypertext, but is a technological latecomer to a society that, in the most profound sense, has always been a Web. Maybe Nietzsche's "spider web" capturing passing victims in its fine-spun silk, but perhaps something else. The American mind was born hypertext: virtual consciousness that from the time of the Pilgrims to the astronauts has enjoyed a unique telematic ability to effortlessly hyperlink between the media-net and personal history. America has always been on-line, because the first rights of American citizenship involve abandoning one's history and past language at the door, recreating personal identity within the pantheon of American mythology. If you don't go on-line America, mixing personal destiny and public events, thinking of America as the "best country in the whole wide world" with yourself as one of the chosen elect no matter what your political quibbles whether to the left or right, you will have no designated site on America's Homepage.

America's Homepage? URL to "The American Dream" on the star spangled power-server at MIT's Media Lab, and multi-media images fantastic suddenly appear on the screen. To the background sound of "The Battle Hymn of the Republic," the screen goes up in red, white, and blue, beginning to flip in a slow loop among process images of the Founding Fathers (no Mothers allowed) of the Republic, traditional heroes of the American Revolution, American Presidents past, present, and virual future, grisly images of Hollywood stars from Babylon Revisited decapitated, burnt, exiled, drug-busted, drug-dead, and drug-joyed, Serial killers, Serial Moms and Dads and Oedipal Kids, and all-time favorite techno gadgetry: wood sidewalled panelled '54 Chevy station wagons, '65 Mustangs deep blue, white interior with that just push me to the floor on the wide-open road Dad look, early 60s stand-alone suburb-perfect stereo sputnik speakers, Cuisinarts and Garborators and "Surrey with the Fringe on Top" lawnmowers, and PC's and Mac's to the hyper, and smart houses in all the Marin Counties of the American Information Superhighway.

Like it or not, America is the digital future. However, the problem is that we no longer have the ability to love it or leave it. America is not just a physical presence, but a virtual space.

ARTIFICIAL LIFE

Warren Padula

THE PREGNANT ROBOT

Hard nipples, soft lips. Nurturing for the 21st century.

She's no robo-cop. She's no Schwarzenegger. A pregnant robot? The mother might be hardwired for the millennium, but the android baby is taking us back to good old-fashioned human flesh. Like an amniotic crystal ball, perhaps the baby is telling us about our future. Not the future virtual, but the future terminal.

Why can't robots have children?

A little humanoid robo-fetus floating in its mother's external womb, no less loved and certainly no less nurtured by the fact that its mother is an android with milk-sucking vacuum pumps for breasts, silicon for a cervical cortex, fiber optic cables wrapped in icey-blue titanium for fingers, and an indefinite network of telemetry for a nervous system. A perfect scene of maternal bliss between baby android and its mother carrier. This image of the pregnant robot welcomes us to the 3rd millennium, to that point where the human species as we have known it disappears, and even human fertility is downloaded into alien bodies. But, perhaps, not so alien: the robot has human lips (a Cindy Crawford smile?), and just a trace of skin across her face. Is this a haunting presence of the human that is intended to emphasize the absence of flesh, or a trace of the disappeared human body that is meant to enhance the cold beauty of the designed body of the robotic woman? And the fetus? It's carried in the remote-powered hands of the robot outside the womb, but it's definitely human. The robot as a future servo-womb for a human species that has displaced motherhood? Or the android baby as the successor species to all the ruling robots?

But maybe there is no pregnant robot, just a psychological

projection in the form of a painterly image of an android mother and baby-in-a-bubble of a double human anxiety: a projective sense of bodily alienation directed to the vanishing of the human species into robo-flesh, and a more retrospective alienation of humans from their own bodies. Or perhaps something else. When the machines finally come alive in the form of flesh-eating technology, we will have achieved not only the end of the human body as we have known it and the end of history, but also the end of pregnancy.

A pregnant robot? Well, if this is our future, it's not so bad. Humans have always been crawling out of their skin on the way to android consciousness, and robots dream every night about giving birth to little humanoids. After all, human skin is the very best android flesh of all.

It's 2:00 a.m. in the morning, and we're thinking about this image of robotic flesh in front of us which might be our door of misperception to Terminal Futures. Recently, we've noticed a lot of cold romance in the air: sudden breakdowns of personalities and bodies and feelings and relationships. This decade has the feel of the 1890s written all over it; not Mahler's melancholia, but a kind of hyper-inversion of that. Sort of a general dementia that's so big and so crazy that it just bursts though the flesh and goes robo-keening. Like this image of a pregnant robot, titled **Introspection.**

SKATING AWAY THE 90S

The 1990s just skated by.

She was dressed in monochrome black: tank top, lycra shorts, Ray Bans and a pulp fiction hairstyle cut at the head with a beautifully hand-tooled emerald colored **Hammerhead** helmet. And all this like a mobile body performance theatre piece for cruising the street scene on some cool looking **Oxygen** inlines, gliding in and out of sun-stalled traffic with the drivers red-faced furious.

Now, I was just standing at the bus stop waiting for the millennium when she stopped to ask the time. When I said: "We're running out of it," she replied, "Hey, don't be a crazy-assed boy toy. If it's time you want, you can always get more of it at **Club Full Throttle.** Check it out."

Which I did that night.

Full Throttle is a hyper-glitter version of a techno-ambient bar somewhere in London that likes to advertise itself as all about "Speed, Power and the Pursuit of Happiness."

The kind of club where you check your in-lines at the door, get green fluorescent ink stamped on the inside of your wrist by heavy-dude muscle bouncers, walk to the bar for a cool-me-down beer which you grip full-fisted by the handle low down by your side, beer just right for fighting or loving, or maybe even drinking. (At least that's what the TV ads say).

Finish the beer, and merge your body into the full throttle dance crowd. Techno music from Italy with Dutch DJ's laying a heavy algorithmic 4/4 track on sweating flesh as we try to fly away to that happy helmet zone in the sky. You know that you're never going to pop out of your skin on your own, so you make your way to the all-hours pharmacy in the basement, pay the going toll to the wired dominatrix at the counter and when she rolls out her wares like an Oedipal family on methadone crystal — Sister Ecstasy, Daddy H and Brother Crack — you go straight for sisterly love and take your celestial pleasures.

A drug-of-the-month tab of E was the arcade favorite that night at **Full Throttle:** Clarity descends from the mega-watt, whomping deep bass speakers. Suddenly, techno music is channelled directly into your blood stream like a multi-sampled rush of colored sound sparkles. It's not even that you're listening to techno anymore, walls of sound just float away like brilliant chunks of liquid crystal, sounds take on shimmering hues, like steel-green and ochre and flash-fire red, and the repetitive techno beat begins to taste like process flesh on a super fast ride through the pixel carnival sideshow.

Later in the morning, when the sun's finally up and your body is finally down, you remember where it all began, with the 90s skating by and that neat in-line visionary telling you that if it's time you want, and maybe even need, get your flesh to **Full Throttle.** She was right, and I never got to thank her. So maybe this is in the way of a little note of appreciation if you're still skating somewhere down the boulevard of smoke and ice.

THE WEDDING DRESS

She was beautiful. He was handsome. She wore a white satin bridal gown, and he a white tuxedo.

We first saw them standing in front of what looked like a large, camouflaged army vehicle. But this was no ordinary military vehicle, because we were visiting the Robotics Institute at Carnegie Mellon University: a real hall of fame for future robo-warfare.

We took a closer look. She was still beautiful and he was still handsome, but this was no ordinary bride and groom on the way to the altar. Her dress was dirty and stained and the tulle of her veil was ripped and frayed. Her shoes were combat boots and her socks, army surplus thick green wool. His tuxedo was splattered with fuel oil, his shoes, although white patent leather, were scuffed and stained, and he had an alpha tester for new AI software products jammed in his tuxedo pocket. Now, we've seen blue brides and pink brides and even green brides, but never dirty brides, or grooms for that matter.

They begin to tell us their story as well as the fabled tale of the "non-personnel" robotic vehicle parked at the Lab. It seems that the CMU lab is the birthing place of America's most media-famous robots: Dante, last seen on global satellite TV tipping over on its side while climbing out of a steaming, belching volcano; the Mars long-range planetary explorer, robots for tunneling inside hot radioactive sites at all the future Chernobyl's, and robots for scrubbing clean toxic industrial wastes.

But the very best of all: an all-automated, gleaming artifical intelligence robotic car for worry-free driving on American freeways future. Like all AI progeny, it doesn't look like much right now. At this stage, the "electronics nervous system" is the thing, and the consumer design will come later. That's why the control electronics are housed in a converted US army vehicle: heavy enough to survive artillery fire, camouflage painted. Just perfect for post-millennial travel in the war zone of America's inner cities.

What's interesting about this robo-carrier is that it has already been thoroughly road-tested. Sent out one dark winter night on its maiden robo-voyage without advance warning on a trip with no human passengers from Erie to Pittsburgh, Pennsylvania, about 200 miles through some of the prettiest and certainly slipperiest and most dangerous driving country in America. And all this without a stop, without an accident, and certainly without an auto-eyebrow being raised by all the passing traffic.

Why the dirty and tattered wedding attire? Why the sinister looking drive-by robotic vehicle?

She was an artist from Kansas. He was an AI researcher from Iowa. They met in Pittsburgh. She grew up sharing her dream space with brides. Her father was a photographer who each Saturday morning would use her bedroom as a backdrop for wedding photographs. Her mother's specialty was baking painstakingly beautiful wedding cakes. Her house smelled of the joys of weddings: flowers, French perfumes, cakes with cream cheese frosting. She had fond memories of this experience. After all, they weren't stuffing corpses in her bedroom.

What is the connection between hot rodding robots and a dirty wedding dress? It could be the reality of artificial perversity. The robo-car with its AI technology has been finally liberated from the lab and now finds itself cruising the Interstate. Feeling in its teledonics all the perverse pleasures of a robo-auto out for a covert spin in a road-testing story of its own artificial making. And the wedding dress?

It has been emancipated from the pure artificial space of the wedding day theme park, allowed to be perverted by time's passing. Speed-degraded by time with such intensity that after only a few days onlookers aren't sure whether the wedding couple is cute or mad.

Wedding dresses and robots with AI electronically bubbling brains have always had this in common. They are both about cocooned, sterile spaces: the closed system rationality of artificial intelligence, and the equally clean, and closed, purity of the wedding dress. Both preserved in artificial space and artificial time, safely immunized from the vicissitudes of life.

And that's really the connection between the dirty, impure wedding dress and the joy-riding robo-car. Refusing closed systems, both welcome perversity: either energizing the sterile space of the wedding day by the degradations of time, or enhancing the closed rationality of artificial intelligence by the crash space of the freeway. Getting down and dirty in America.

And you know something? It turns out that this doesn't destroy robotics nor exit weddings, but actually energizes artificial life. The story of the robot and the wedding dress, then, as important theory simulators preparing us for a future of artificial perversity. Artificial perversity? This just might be America's last and best contribution to reinventing digital reality.

Colin and Leah Piepgras

ICE BLUE

She was ice blue
Bluer than blue
Slippery as ice
Cold as satin
Scanning memory
for a trick, a gesture
She was no cyborg charmer.

Blue hair cropped short to her head
she wore a skimpy satin
skirt over bulky sweat-pants
Her baby tee clung to her thin body.
She couldn't stop moving, rocking
from side to side. She never looked
you in the eye.

Ice Blue was at **Cry**
a moveable theme park party
on the industrial outskirts of Frankfurt
a moody moonlight scene of
high-tech ruins of the future
that made me think of Sartre
and his prophecy of the coming
of the serial self
no reciprocity
no recognition

no other
just a bunker self
shut down in a cold cell of waiting time.
Not hell is other people
but hell is myself like a great, big autistic scream.
Ice Blue
spell-bound in a hypnotic rhythm
all by herself
splayed right in front of the DJ
silver stilettos
a real trance-head
chanting again and again
"Process. Excess. Surface.
Liquid Delirious Material.
Cyber-Life on a Spin."
"Process. Excess. Surface.
Liquid Delirious Material.
Cyber-Life on a Spin."
"Process. Excess. Surface.
Liquid Delirious Material.
Cyber-Life on a Spin."

THE SCREAMING TREE
AN *ELECTRONIC FABLE*

I once knew an artist
actually a Princess,
who loved "treeness"
but not trees,
flowerness
but not flowers,
greenness
but not grass,
humanity
but not people

She had all the money in the world
She was the Princess of the digital woods
One day she awoke
and decided she wanted to make
the art of "treeness"
the sounds of treeness
the codes of treeness
the interfaces of treeness
the soft images of treeness

So she gathered in her new age electronic court
all the most famous artists in the kingdom
the best composers and designers and programmers.
When they were assembled there,
the Princess came down from her wired throne

and said:
"GIVE ME TREENESS"
So the artists went back to their studios
and began to have visions of treeness.
In early spring,
just as the leaves were budding
on the trees
they returned to the electronic court of the Princess
with wires and multi-media graphical interfaces,
MIDI processors, digital scans, recombinant images,
hard disks, ram, device-drivers,
and 3D accelerators, just oozing with treeness.

And the Princess said:
"This is good. You have discovered with my guidance
true treeness.
But we must take our true treeness
to the oldest tree in the woods
the wise old oak tree".

And so they did
They hard-wired the old oak tree.
Soon,
sounds and images and texts of true treeness
became the digital sap of the old oak tree.
But what sounded good at the digital court
sounded horrid in the woods
kitschy and silly
whimpy, foolish, and sorry

Because
between true treeness and the trees
between soft(ware) oak and hard oak
between dry codes and the organic tree
between the Princess and her fabulous dreams
there was **oak wetware** — an interface problem:
For no one asked the oak tree
if it liked digital codes for sap
computer networks for branches
pixel leaves
a recombinant memory of seasonal changes or,
What is the the sound of a falling oak in a digital forest
if no microminions are around?

The Princess was angry
looking up at the old oak tree, she screamed:
"WHERE IS MY TREENESS?"
"You can't buy treeness with money, my Princess,"
said the old oak tree.
"To find true treeness, you must look to the trees!"

THE THIRD RIGHT
HACKING THE AMERICAN WAY

That's Newt Gingrich's
"A Magna Carta for the Knowledge Age"
where Newt and the boys want
to hack the future
They want to tame it, train it
and hack it for profit
where Alvin Toffler wants his third
wave to drown us out
so he can go fishing in
cyberspace for
coaxial cables, dark fiber, and digital hardware
"It's our turn," they all chant
to download, upload, freeload
and explode what they call
"Cyberspace and the New American Dream."
But we call it a Nightmare
nothing between the underclass
and the virtual class,
No public control
just virtual elites,
Certainly no liberty for all
just Newt and the boys in a
perfect little techno-bubble
clean, sterile and immunized
from degrading American flesh
Be wired, they say

Get deregulated and upgraded
Get netted and vetted
Get multi-tasked, demassified and bit-netted
Get backslashed, backtracked and backlit
Let's surf, merge, and purge
Leave behind the First and Second Waves
and welcome the famous Third Wave

DIGITAL FLESH

Paul Winternitz

0 / S

Digital Flesh? That's life in the 90s as a transitional time when we are stuck with 20th century flesh in 21st century hypertext minds. Alternatively frightening and exciting, we are perhaps the last of the human species born without data skin or cyber-organs. Unlike the *fin-de-siecle* generation of the 1890s who experienced feelings of anxiety and melancholy over the dawning of the modern age, the fin-de-millennium generation gives itself over to feelings of cold romance. Why drown in the wetware of the body organic when with a little hollowing out, hardening, and drying up as Stelarc likes to say, the body telemetic can appear on the scene ready for life in the 3rd millennium? Our generation cannot be nostalgic about the disappearance of the organic body because, unlike the 1890s, we have never lived with the illusion of the real. For us, the "reality" of the flesh was the first casualty of life in the 20th century.

Body nostalgia is a terrible thing, particularly since we have long ago lost sight of where the body is actually located. Inhabited by pulsing electronic currents, written by language, space-bound by the pressures of class, ideology, and race, policed by the Daddy's "No," the body shatters into a rainbow spectrum of brilliant shards of glistening ice flesh. The desiring body, the sexed body, the techno-body, the consumer body, the narcotized body, the working body, the disciplined body: what is real or unreal? Who possesses the body? And who is possessed by the dreams forbidden of a body that floats across its multiple diffractions?

Perhaps the lost utopia of a body that never existed accounts for the seduction of digital reality. Not a will to abandon the body that never actually existed, but a will to gather together all the nostalgia for the lost referent of the body into a new architecture of the virtual body. A virtual Shangri-la: that's the digital algorithm. The nostalgic desire to recuperate the body vanished into a new combinatorial of emergent senses. Definitely not a product of the desire to exit the body, digital flesh is exactly the opposite. It's the desire to relocate the certainty of the body, if only virtually, in opposition to the dispersion of flesh into vectors of speed. A brilliant manifestation of the will to purity, the digital algorithm is a futile, but no less tragic, search for the pure body equipped with an electronic repertoire of improved emergent senses.

Not something new, digital reality continues anew a very ancient story: the struggle between two irreconcilable elements in the human drama—the unwanted reality of the decay of the flesh, and the long-dreamed promised land of escape from the body organic to the pure, technological body. Between the necessity of bodily corruption and exiting human flesh, that's the utopia *and* futility of digital reality.

Now this story has been told before. It's endemic to human mythology. Everyone has passed this way before: Greek enlightenment, Christian confessionality, cultural atomists, fascist eugenics, social engineering, the aestheticized body of Platonists, physiocrats, pantheists, positivist rationality, and pure linguistics.

In the future, when digital reality is just another sad 90s multimedia CD-ROM on the historical shelf, people may look back and nod their heads with a mixture of awe and contempt at the pretensions of fin-de-millennium culture that thought for one brief, utopian, futurist-driven moment that it could do what no era had every accomplished before: to actually escape the curse of time-binding history, finally unlocking the ancient Riddle of the Sphinx.

WINDOWS ON WHAT?

It's a hot day in July '95 and I'm tuned into cyber-business, reading a feverish newspaper report of "Glee at Microsoft as the master version of Windows 95 is finally shipped." The mood in Redmond, Washington is ecstatic, like a last day of cyber-school party, as the coder fraternity gets together for a victory bash: drinking Dom Perignon, diving into the fountain, spraying whipped cream, maybe a game or two of pin the tail on Bill Gates' donkey, and, who knows, even spin the bottle. Thinking I haven't noticed it reading over my shoulder, my PC slinks away into the next room and suddenly starts to cough with the rasping sound of a summer algorithmic cold. I can already hear it whining for a Win 95 upgrade.

My micro-joy is abruptly terminated by TV scenes from Srebrenica. It seems that when the UN declared Srebrenica, Tuzla and Gorazde as "safe areas," it forgot to tell the Bosnian Muslims that it meant safe **only** for the UN. For the Muslims, the so-called safe areas are actually temporary holding depots, hospices where the UN collects refugees from ethnically cleansed areas in order to hand them over en masse to the Bosnian Serbs on demand. When the Government of Bosnia-Herzegovina does a bit of truth-telling, declaring the UN soldiers to be on a wilderness camping trip, diplomats and officers throw their hands in the air, deploring the lack of "political will" and calling for just one more meeting. Sunday afternoon barbeques in the West are spliced with TV images from the all too real theme park of suffering in Bosnia: hungry children, suicided women, raped girls, and lynched and stoned and knifed men and boys.

Harold Innis, a Canadian theorist, once said that the ultimate bitterness is to have consciousness of much and the ability to do nothing about it. Like the TV consciousness of the genocide of Bosnian Muslims that takes place this minute, and the world is silent. Clinton stalls for time as he checks his radar for signs of political damage. Pentagon Generals flank the American Secretary of Defense as he repeats the official (exaggerated) rhetoric: "The Bosnian 'quagmire' will involve at least 200,000 American ground troops. We'll only fight in the air." Of course, when the French ask for air support in the form of helicopter gunships, Clinton says he'll get back to them later. With a survey for a conscience, Clinton is the perfect representative American politician at the end of the century: playing a waiting game while rolling the dice of moral appeasement. Kohl burps, Major smirks, Chretien golfs, and we stumble. Boutros Boutros-Ghali plays the Maitre D' of international panel discussions, and Chirac, with cynicism on his side, demands military intervention in Bosnia while planning to nuke the South Pacific.

It's no use blaming the political leaders without shame or a UN without courage because we're all complicit. It's also **our** moral genocide that's taking place in Bosnia. Knowledge met with indifference indicates an inner appeasement: a moral settlement of our own ethical conscience on the lower terms of the pragmatism of futility, if not disinterest. An earlier generation responded to the crisis of the Spanish Civil War by recognizing historical events for what they were — the first appearance in the 20th century of fascism on European soil. They formed the International Brigades which, if they weren't ultimately victorious on the military field, marked the outer frontier, the irrevocable "No," that first-generation fascism was never able to transgress.

It's our turn now. Second-generation fascism lives again in the form of the Bosnian Serbs. What will be the response of our generation? A moral assent to evil by tuning out Bosnia and turning off TV? Or, following Camus, an earlier traveller on the road against fascism, might it be possible that we'll remember his fateful words addressed to the survivors of the 20th century: "I rebel, therefore **we** exist." Time now for the 2nd International.

CLOSING DOWN THE REAL WORLD/
OPENING UP THE VIRTUAL WORLD

It is no coincidence that the "shipping out" of Windows 95 and the fall of Srebrenica take place on the same weekend. These are deeply entwined events. What takes place in Redmond and Srebenica is the final settlement of human flesh in the last days of the 20th century: the bitter division of the world into virtual flesh and surplus flesh. Windows 95 opens out onto the dominant ideology and privileged life position of digital flesh. It installs the new codes of the master occupants of virtual worlds: frenzied devotion to cyber-business, life in a multi-media virtual context, digital tunnel vision, and, most of all, embedded deep in the cerebral cortex of the virtual elite an **I-chip:** I, that is, for complete indifference. Technological acceleration is accompanied by a big shutting-down of ethical perception.

Windows 95 might be very good for file management, multi-tasking, and games for your head with nothing on your mind, but it tells us nothing about Srebrenica. And why should it?

In technology as in life, every opening is also a closing, and what is closed down by the tech hype of Windows 95 is consciousness of surplus flesh. That's Srebrenica: the surplus flesh of Bosnian Muslims who do not have anything to contribute to virtual worlds: fit subjects only to be ethnically, and physically, disappeared. They can be ethnically cleansed because they have first been **technically cleansed.** They are surplus to world domination in a cyber-box.

CYBER SEX

When I was in Berlin recently, I met a young American hacker who was living in Europe, much like a virtual descendant of the lost generation of America of the 1920s. Rather than flee to the literary and artistic scene of the Paris that was then or to Prague, the new romantic Paris of the 1990s, the new lost generation of America is fast disappearing into all the virtual reality labs of the European information superhighway. He told me that he was from suburban Connecticut, one of those tract interzones that have no real name, only a highway express exit, no means of social solidarity, only a depressing sense of electronic solitude, and, finally, no communication, just groups of friends that get together only to watch a video. This hacker had fled the impossible inner loneliness of the American individual for the techno-scene of Europe, and was in the process of recomposing himself virtually. Researching at the furthest forward edge of cybernetics, he was creating wonderful substitution-effects for every aspect of the social experience that he had never had: cyber-feeling, cyber-eyes, cyber-touching, and, most of all, cyber-sex. He might have fled America because of the inner loneliness of the American self, but he was actually creating a virtual self, probably for immediate export back to the USA.

He told me an interesting story about his own experience with cyber-sex. It seemed that he and a French hacker had created two total-immersion body suits, algorithmically just right for long-distance sexual feeling. Distributive sex for the age of distributive intelligence and distributive feeling. A perfect cyber-sex machine in which you slip into the virtual flesh of the data suit in Paris or Berlin, and have a remote sexual experience with a person, friend or stranger it doesn't make much difference, who has zipped into the other data body. Now, this cyber-sex experiment was widely publicized as a virtual art event, attracting enormous crowds in Paris and Berlin. For two days, long lines of Europeans eager to distribute their sexual feelings to long-distance hosts waited impatiently for this opportunity to engage in cyber-sexual takeoff. People vectored their bodies into the cyber-sex suits, toggled the switches, and were reported in various stages of sexual ecstacy as they felt licks and touches and probes from partners who might have been telematically remote, but who were intensely virtually intimate.

However, a curious thing happened. At the end of the second day, the hacker's cyber-partner from Paris sent a message to say that there was a big coding problem. It seemed that a cyber-glitch in the programming had occured at the Paris end of things, and that the system was running on a closed feedback loop. What this meant was that when you zipped on the data suit and plugged into all the waiting orifices of the long-distance remote partner, what you were actually feeling was not a virtual person in Berlin or Paris, but your own body. And it felt great! After all, who knows better how to make you feel good than yourself. The European experiment in cyber-sex had turned into a brilliantly autistic feast in cyber-masturbation.

The young American hacker in Berlin was the latest victim of European hubris. He thought he was free of American loneliness, suburban style, only to find himself dumped into the electronic solitude of the masturbating body. Back to Connecticut, back to Blockbuster Video!

GLINT CHIP EYE

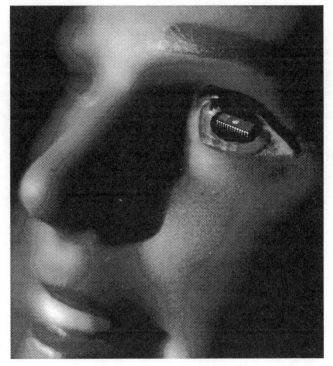

Leif Harmsen

The body electronic comes fully equipped with a glint chip eye for rapid 3D acceleration across the digital galaxy. Advertised as just perfect for texture-mapping, depth-queuing, anti-aliasing, and more realistic rendering of 48 mb of D-RAM, the glint chip eye has the Midas touch of "scalability." Located at the very top of the neuro-skull, the eye electronic has total 360 degree vision, horizon to virtual horizon. It's the electronic eye that finally blinks open to a universe of floating organs.

And why not? It's never known a terrestrial world, and never been dragged down into the gravity of the liquid body by the strangling thread of the optic nerve. Born for a universe of virtualities and modelled effects, the glint chip eye has always only known the speed and violence of 3D imagery.

No bifocals or trifocals needed here
Never closing
Never sleeping
Never requiring prosthetics like **Oliver Peoples** glasses.
an eye electronic without myopia or detached retinas
or glaucoma or hardened lenses
finally liberated from the cosmetology
of eyelashes and eyebrows
the glint chip eye opens to a 3D world
of artificial life, animated memory, and digital optics

Maybe it needs some artificial tears.

THE WORLD WIDE WEB SELF

Tired of ascii consciousness?

Leif Harmsen

Try out a World Wide Web self. That's the body electronic equipped for fast travel across the World Wide Web: neuro skin, URL exo-skeleton with HTML navigational beacons coded into its processing sensor. The WWW self has never known any future but intensive immersion in the force-field of data. A species type born in the age of hyper-text philosophy and neuro-theory, the electronic body speaks only multi-media navigational languages: Mosaic, El Net, Netscape. Perfect navigational tools for an electronic body that has already been resequenced into a data probe with a global positioning system fused into its brain tissue.

ALT.LAST.SEX

Alt.Last.Sex is Berlin's most charismatic under-ground cyber-club for third sex bodies: bodies drifting in a nowhere state between digital flesh and liquid bodily pleasures.

It's virtual location is a secret, but if you down-load into one of the ascii warehouses squatted by the Berlin counter-culture matrix you might luck into the access codes. In the Berlin underground these days, squatting dark fibre is all the rage. Dark fibre? That's surplus ethernet

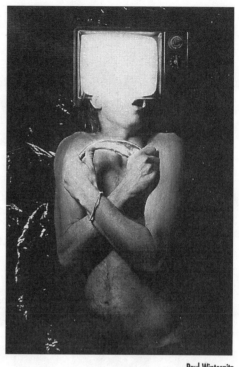

Paul Winternitz

that the planners of cyber-Berlin have installed for future har-vesting. Now at a squat very much like "Tacheles" on Oranienburger StraBe, dark fibre has been accessed by the vir-tual lovers of Alt.Last.Sex.

So if you're feeling lonely, just go up on the Net, Web over to the neural networks of Alt.Last.Sex, and you'll suddenly find yourself in the Berlin underground: floating by the dark labyrinth of Potsdammer Platz with its lonely subway station next to the Fuehrer's bunker, push on past the Brandenberg Gate, do one last check ot your fibre optic flesh with its glassy light array and morph into Alt.Last.Sex.

The night we were there was bubbling vulvas:

Shannon, the ejaculating woman
Orlan, the human vivisection-machine
Toni Denise, the Web's first virtual transexual
Claudia, a franchise operator of a chain of dungeons
Kate, America's most literate transexual who likes to say
"I was a man and then I was a woman, and now I'm neither."
And Stelarc with his third hand and high-energy skin

Bitch Diva was our host. She spent ten years singing manly showtunes on the US club circuit, before she gave it all up for Berlin. With her wigs, beaded dresses, high heels and that sultry voice, she was a real success. And what a bitch!

The song of choice that night was James Brown's "I'm a Sex Machine." Which was just right: a real man talking about real sex, or was it?

THE LIQUID EYE

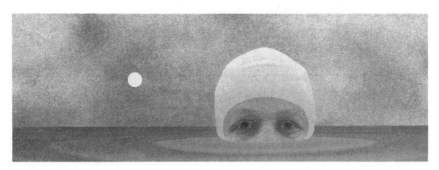

Alex Colville

Marshall McLuhan may be the patron saint of wired culture and processed world, but Alex Colville is the painter of virtual reality.

Leaving behind the fixed point-of-view of Euclidean space and abandoning the realist subordination of modern art, Colville paints the present from the future perspective of the 21st century. Probably against his own intentions and certainly against his rhetoric that seeks to downplay the imminent violence in all of his work, Colville's artistic imagination has broken through to the next millennium. With a singular resolution of aesthetic purpose and an almost frenzied commitment to understand the perspectival prison-house of human experience, Colville paints the architecture of the virtual body. His artistic oeuvre "images" in advance a floating, hyperreal world in which "ordinary experience" — heads, bodies, cats, dogs, rats, birds, horses, boats — are always already aesthetic after-images of mathematically constructed spaces. A painter of and for the future, Colville's art is a visual record of a (human) history already experienced, but not yet understood.

In Colville's world, mathematics becomes flesh, a measured space where the new math of saddle curves and parabolic field-events jumps out of the theory textbooks and colonizes the body with such intensity that flesh implodes, becoming an aesthetic after-image of architectural logic. Fleshy remainder, cancelled faces, floating bodily silhouettes: it's as if the construction of the virtual image-system comes first, and flesh is then painted onto the invisible algorithmic surfaces as an impossibly seductive sign of the illusion of humanity. An architectural world, then, of visible flesh and invisible mathematical symmetry. A painterly galaxy of virtual reality effects where the act of perspectival mapping is sovereign, and the imaged body is brought into presence only as a beautiful, yet eerie, sign of its own disappearance.

Consider **Swimmer and Sun.** A haunting painting precisely because of its game of the doubled other. The aesthetic mapping is deceptively simple: a fluorescent sun in the background, the swimmer's head in the privileged foreground, a perfect plane of water with planetary ripples spreading out from the head like the swirls in the Milky Way, no shadows (this is only a virtual space), and gathering storm clouds on the horizon as an intimation of the catastrophe that has already occured.

Two planetary orbs: the sun and the swimmer's head. But which is the real sun? And which is the real head? The swimmer's head has no existence other than that of an illusion of pure mathematics, a perspectival after-effect as the radiating centre of a liquid universe. It's the same for the fluorescent sun: a constructed image that glows brightly in the background as a reminder of a natural scene that does not exist. The sun, therefore, as the swimmer's head of an illusional physical universe; and the swimmer's head as the brilliant sun of virtual humanity. Two suns, and two heads also: a perfect similitude of signs of a universe that exists only as an aesthetic trompe l'oeil. Thus, a game of the doubled other where swimmer and sun conspire in a parody of signs to pretend that something exists, if only the illusion of naturalism.

Maybe **Swimmer and Sun** is a painterly remembrance of Bataille in **The Solar Anus**:

> Everyone is aware that life is parodic and
> lacks an interpretation.
> Thus lead is the parody of gold.
> Air is the parody of water.
> The brain is the parody of the equator.
> Coitus is the parody of crime. *

In **Swimmer and Sun**, the head only breaks the surface of the water to announce the bleak truth of the future of the virtual head: a mute sight-machine in which the eye is privileged, but the orifice of the mouth is silenced. Here, there is no communication, only the floating eye as a liquid sign of the virtual body's disappearance into an optical after-effect. No social solidarity, only a virtual head moving in a liquid orbit with its fluorescent double of the twilight sun. And certainly no memory, since the silencing of the mouth intimates the suffocation of the fleshly body below the plane of the water. Our virtual future then: a vacant sight-machine frozen in a liquid galaxy of virtual signs.

Swimmer and Sun is a perfect visual tombstone for the twilight time of the 20th century, and an equally evocative warning in advance of the reprise of the human condition into the pleasuredome of virtuality in the dawning millennium.

---

* G. Bataille, *Visions of Excess: Selected Writings 1927-1939*, Minneapolis, University of Minnesota Press, 1985, p.5.

ARCADE COWBOY

We are the people of the third millennium.

Einstein's children born in the white flash of nuclear exterminism, retro-fitted for the VR arcades. For us, relativity theory, the search for the top quark of quantum mechanics, and the lonely spin of pulsars in deep space have always been our primal nature.

As we come under the pull of the Year 2000, you can almost feel the shifting of generations: mid-20th century body models might have modernist nervous systems

Leif Harmsen

but sometimes manage to break through to postmodern technology, Slackers and those of the so-called Generation X were born postmodern but are still part of the chip generation oscillating between flesh and data. Now there's an entirely new generation: the digital generation. Post-chip, pure digital wonders of the 3rd millennium.

SUICIDE DRIVE

It's midnight and I'm at Pier 39 on the shores of the Pacific in San Francisco. Hottest VR games just in from Tokyo are hard-wired to the consoles, and you can go for some really cool rides: **Megadeath**, **Kung Fu Warriors**, **Neo-Geo**, **Virtual Fighters;** where you take your jet fighter squadron out over the Atlantic, straight off the deck of bucking aircraft carriers. Or for the newest cyber-game to be copied to the Californian mind, try **Suicide Drive**, and race a Formula 1 gleaming red Mitsubishi convertible at 200 kliks around the streets of Monte Carlo. Remember Bruce Lee in **Enter the Dragon**? Well there's no need now to get bruised and bloodied, let alone have a heart-attack before you're thirty. The worst you can expect with these cyber-games is a little VR nausea or perhaps a few psycho-flashbacks.

I'm cyber-drifting Pier 39 in the company of Star, a student from the local art college. He's introduced to me as an electronic artist who a year ago went on a field trip with his class to Pier 39 and never came back from the cyber-arcades. He calls himself an arcade cowboy, and from dawn to dusk plays the game. From his four long black braids and Stetson to his silver-tipped cowboy boots, he's ready to ride the cyber-matrix on the shores of the Pacific, just where the waves of the ocean meet the 3rd wave generation of VR players.

When I ask him what he likes best about the cyber-matrix, he says: "It's way better than sex. Sex is disease, but machines are so clean."

He's my very first apparition of the third millennium.

Now Pier 39 that night was a real fuzzy force-field. Big Daddies with babies strapped to their backs were hammering away at judo fighting machines. And the babies? Well they looked over their Papa's shoulders at the flickering screens and you could almost feel the twitching of little fingers as they practiced their video machine strokes.

African-Americans splayed themselves before screens filled with Japanese video warriors: a strange switching of races as bodies are fast-processed through the imagery. And all the while fierce four-member packs of VR arcade guards, suited up as simu-California state troopers, watch.

And Star? Away from the electronic force-field, his body fades away into inertia: limp, lifeless, almost autistic, a junk body with the energy turned off just like electronic performance art when it's powered-down and gone terminal. But then he steps up to **Mortal Kombat**, and the cyber-dude hidden in his shadowy self bursts right out, his fingers seem to grow prosthetic flexors all the better for machine flexibility, and his body motions are pure digital reality: smooth, sinewy, hardwired, more algorithmically focussed and speed-processed than human flesh was ever meant to be.

Someone leans over and asks him in the middle of a frenzied game. "Do you think you could just walk away from this game if you really wanted to?

His instant reply. "Sure, as long as I get to win first."

JOHNNY MNEMONIC:
THE DAY CYBERPUNK DIED

Johnny Mnemonic, the movie, is the day when cyberpunk died.

It's failure is interesting less for aesthetic reasons — acting, screenplay, cinemetography, special effects — than for what it says about the hyper-modern mind and its taste for shifting cultural signs. Killed by sheer cultural acceleration, by the fact that 80s cyberpunk metaphors don't really work anymore in the virtual 90s, the popular failure of **Johnny Mnemonic** testifies to the end of the charismatic phase of digital reality, and the beginning of the iron law of technological normalization. In the age of **Neuromancer** we could still believe for one charismatic moment that the body could deep-dish its way past screenal telemetry into galactic flows of data, that Molly could vamp her way to mind fusion, that Case could jump out of his flesh and byte-fry his way to Starlight, that somehow we could become data, and it would be good.

Now **Neuromancer** hit just when high-tech was in its charismatic state of innocent grace, still a crazy fusion of computer visionaries and outlaw businessmen and hacker writers coming in for a moment from the back alleys of the digital frontier to check out the daytime scene with all the suspenders in the software labs. Like all cultural movements before it, tech charisma lasts for only one brief, shining instant, and then it fades away into the grim sociology of rationalized technology or, failing which, it quickly disappears from life. The lessons of the 90s have been multiple and they've been harsh: not the least of which is that data will find a way, and it's way is not necessarily about becoming human. While the charisma of tech will never be retrieved again, its memory lingers on the horizon like a beautiful beckoning dream, all the more seductive for its absence.

And **Johnny Mnemonic**? The movie suffers the very worst fate of all: it's been normalized, rationalized, chopped down to image-consumer size, drained of its charisma and recuperated as a museum-piece of lost cybernetic possibilities. Perhaps that's why the film provokes such intense resentment among the cyber-crowd. Its presence is a bitter reminder of the decline of cyberpunk into the present state of hyper-rational (hyper-marketplace) technology. And cyberpunk? It will remain a permanent part of the American literary landscape as a simulation of sci-fi transgression, but only in the doubled form of the transgression that confirms. That's **Johnny Mnemonic**, the difference that recuperates: a cinematic tombstone for the cyberpunk that was its own creation.

M. Kroker,
BERLIN, 1995

TECH FLESH

For too long, skin has had it easy. A passive container for holding together all the organs and blood and water and pus and bones and muscle of the body, skin has never had to press itself, been stressed out, or even had to think. Like an evolutionary hanger-on from an earlier age, skin has gone along for the ride. Big, fat, and lazy: a epidermal slacker before its time.

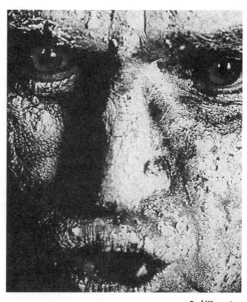

Paul Winternitz

In digital reality, all that's about to change. Now is the time of intelligent, distributive skin that abandons its loyalty to localized bodies and goes electronic. Algorithmic skin that refuses its assigned evolutionary default position of being a passive container for the organic body, becoming environmentally challenged. Philosophical/working skin that actively senses its environment, acts as a photosynthesizing agent for quick energy transfers for the body redesigned, and sometimes even serves as a hologramic screen for the mutating identities of body shifters. Tech flesh for the 21st century.

Skin's had it easy? Never. It's been scorched and burned and pockmarked, puckered, blemished and blistered, cut, sliced and tortured. Stretched tight over fat thighs and bulging stomachs, skin has been the hateful target of all bulimics, and the first defense against germs. Think about it the next time you sit on a toilet seat.

TERMINAL DANCE

We're having dinner with Edouard Lock, the choreographer of La La La Human Steps, Montreal's full-muscled, psycho-techno dance company, and leading coders at a local Montreal Microsoft branch-plant that specializes in multi-media, graphical interfaces. It's a subdued affair because against all expectations it comes hard on the cyber-heels of a bitter defeat of machinic logic by the dancer's body. None of the coders are particularly eager to tell the tale and, in fact, the Midi Processors had been invited to dinner but for some reason begged off at the last moment. It seems that just last week La La La Human Steps had been invited by the software hackers to participate in an artistic experiment right at the envelope of aesthetic creativity and hacking the 3D imaging future. The idea was a bold one, probably inspired by the coder motif to go where no dancer had gone before: to sequence the super fast, muscular trademark motions of La La La Human Steps by super sophisticated graphical 3D imaging processors, and then to sequence back the images in a recombinant loop with some added android modifications. The dancers' bodies would be forced to go into hyper-motion, sequenced dancing moving finally at the speed of machines. And, who knows, in the usual perverse trick that multimedia programmers like to play on dancers, La La La Human Steps might be force-choreographed into a future where dancers would be made to perform to a virtual machinic logic that would display all the inadequacies of human flesh before the impossible (bodily) perspectives of digital reality.

However, a funny thing happened on the way to the image processors. Strapping on bus ports and bubble memory arrays, the dancers from La La La Human Steps dropped out of their everyday flesh and hard-rammed their bodies into a liquid psycho dance. Flipping into hyper-speed, their bodies dissolved into vehicular blurs of high-intensity motion. And nothing polite about it either. They **vomit** the human condition. This was spew dancing: a manic dance that longs to go terminal, and when it does, it flips us inside out and lets out in one big body scream all the violence and envy and hatred and cheating and friction and lust that are the system operating codes of digital times. Well, the waiting banks of image processors had never seen anything like it, and they were morally shocked, just turned off. Like a prim and prissy church group that likes to gossip its way to the Presbytery on Sundays for an evening of virtual religion lite, the computers were used to the soft rhythmic flows of New Age dance.

What's worse, the graphical sensory arrays of the Midi Processors couldn't keep up to the warp jump speed of the psycho dancers. Computational loops began to alias and displace in random electronic discharges, vague vectors of speed bodies floated across the screens, and just when the image processors finally heaved a telematic sigh that they were finally catching up to terminal times, well, at that point, La La La Human Steps went speed crazy, just body vector mad, and blasted off into a high-arc orbit of pure topological dance. Dancers' bodies as vectors of light, jerking, pounding limbs as smoking trails of speed in the screenal sky, and mantra chanting of "vector, vector, speed, speed, die, die, loop, loop" just pushing down tight muscles into their body sockets and then exploding outwards like heavy-recoil weapons.

In the end, it was just too much. Confused and angry and repulsed and humiliated, the image banks crashed and crashed and crashed. On that day, at least, the will to virtuality had met its bodily match in some possessed dancers from La La La Human Steps who just couldn't be stuffed into the machines for future mounting.

Human Species-1; Digital Reality-0.

FLESH HACKERS

We recently visited a biogenetics lab in Boston, right off Route 128 ("America's Technology Highway"). The project of the day at the lab was producing digital flesh in a Petri dish.

Responding to the Baby Boomers' panic demand for massive doses of drugs to ward off the first signs of the aging process, the biogenetics lab did the pharmaceutical industry one better. The lab was in the process of unlocking the genetic code for wrinkle-free skin: baby fresh flesh that could be guaranteed wrinkle-free until the age of seventy-five, and that as a bonus (flesh) track also would be immunized against unsightly blemishes, blotched skin, and age spots from all those fun in the sun summers.

Figuring that this was an easier road to cut than cosmetic surgery with its TV images terrifying of black eyes and bruised skin and short-circuited nerves, we had ourselves injected immediately. Flapping our bodies weary down on the medical tables and begging for an early shot of improved biogenetic flesh, we were happy experimental subjects renewing the body for a better day. And it was truly an experience: body morphing on the eastern seaboard. Firm flat bellies, skin with the elasticity and color hues of teenage flesh past, heightened cheekbones, vanishing wrinkles, and even some real flesh-shifters as previously sagging skin resynched into its prescribed biogenetic alignment. Those photoshop faces beautiful in **Vanity Fair** had nothing on us: like flesh pioneers of old, we had become living, walking Petri dishes for the biogenetics lab. And we were mighty proud of it.

Of course, it was all a one-day techno-Boston wonder. When we awoke the next morning, the instant simskin effects had vanished and we were abandoned to our bodies remorseful and aging. But it didn't really matter. Like struggling flesh that had been to the mountaintop, we had seen, not the Lord, but that shining sunshine of freedom from the ruins of the body. For one delicious moment, we had shed our skin like human snakes and quick-morphed our way by a little biogenetic procedure into the body in a magic bubble. Now we knew that we would probably never get to the promised land of wrinkle-free skin, emergent skin, but, dear Lord Almighty, we had seen the light, the magnificent light, of theme park flesh. Like a replay of the more ancient struggle between senescence and redemption, but this time with an upbeat conclusion, we had actually experienced in the digital flesh the pleasures of the fully recombinant face, the cloned body, the sampled nervous tissue. Thrown back into the hell of living flesh, we would always think again in the years to come of that one brief moment off Route 128, America's Technology Highway, when we actually became the theme park body, resurrected flesh in a bubble for a single day and night. We were flesh hackers, and while it would not be for us to enjoy the promised land, we could point the way for other skin voyagers on their digital pilgrimage.

SCANNER

Scanner's in town from London, and the outlaw cyber-crowd driftworks its way to **No Innocence**, a dance bar on the corner of boul. St-Laurent and Prince Arthur in Montreal. It's the usual kind of 21st century medieval bar gone recombinant: blue lights, particularly in the toilets and stairwell, so that patrons can't see their veins when trying to shoot up heroin, stagey gothic shields of stained glass and iron fifteen-feet wide on the ceiling, dungeon walls, belching woofers of artificial smoke (probably to dry out our oral secretions all the faster and thus sell more beer). And the crowd was great, a real bodily pitch-bender: some were there for the trance music, others for filling up the orifices of hungry cyber-ears, and yet others seemed to just want to travel with Scanner to that nowhere state of death-head ambient sound cut with the sudden static bursts of live scans of the city's electronic envelope.

Scanner appears on the high altar of the DJ stage six feet above the dance floor, surrounded by smoke and strobes and mesmerized scanner flesh fans. The music was fantastic. Not just for the warps and blends and displacements and time-compressions of the forbidding dark anti-melodic sounds, but also for what wasn't there in the sound architecture: no 4/4 rock beat, but an unpredictably phase-shifted sound to produce dance music perfect for our android future. And profoundly emotional too: deep displacements of heavy sounds five octaves down are randomly cut with live scanner electronic discharges.

pimps and prostitutes
sex lines and cops
hospital emergency rooms
suburban chatter and night-time dream voices and
runaway express trains
heading straight for a date with the atrocity museum,
but most of all,
just plain folks, bitching and pushing and shoving and cyber-
grovelling and whining across the field of the electronic sky,
trying to get through one more night,
trying to connect in an empty galaxy of dead sound.

For one cabalistic moment of scanner magic, the **No Innocence** crowd stops dancing, the chatter suddenly falls silent, and even Scanner steps away from his midi processor. We're all caught up in an electronic nowhere trance, drifting at the edge of scanner sounds that our bodily registers are not equipped to pick up with normal bio-sensors and the deep bass phasal-shifted cyber-thunder of Scanner's musical reply to the electronic sonic gods of cyber-city. We realize that we're practitioners of a more ancient religious festival, cyber-ears opened up by the tech voodoo of Scanner to primal sounds for the electronic age.

We shake our heads to clear out the electronic spell that's invaded bodily flesh, look at Scanner and are stunned to see that his skin is washed in a silver-tinted glaze. We think these surely are slide images projected on his skin and shaven head, but then look around to discover that Scanner's a musician of tech flesh. Given the right circumstances and the right auditory mood, he doesn't just do live scanner performances, but he actually becomes a scanning machine. Random images of his past and probably of ours too begin to metamorphose on his flesh like 3D hologramic images, seduced out of their hiding-place in the body by the siren-call of electronic discharges until they leak outwards onto Scanner's skin, like beautifully mutating sonic spores. It's a truly spectacular sight: images of a ten-year-old boy (that's the early Scanner) hanging a microphone from his bedroom window to capture the sounds of passing cars which are then played back with a ten-second delay, panic scenes of pilots having their very last scan by waiting airplane recorders as they sequence into a crash-scene, John Cage and Scanner caught up in floating sonic drift as noise flips between the extremes of idle boredom and excess speech.

And it's just the way it should be because Scanner has never been interested in noise and certainly not in music as much as he's obsessesed with voices disappearing into the electronic vortex: voices with working class accents, voices neutered to fit upper-class body types, voices that come right out of the soil of the British midlands, American midwest or Chiba City — voices cut and spliced and randomly discharged across the cellular telephone net, abuse voices, seductive voices, no-go dead voices on all the desperate answering- and phone sex machines of the world.

M. Kroker

AFTERSCAN

It's 3:00 a.m. and the cyber-party at **No Innocence** is over. We all gather at Fear's apartment in Old Montreal for a millennial version of the good old jam session. Except this time nobody pulls out an instrument. All the composers reach for their DAT tapes, flip scanner selections into a black Cuisinart of a machine, and settle back for a pure exchange of scanner sounds: a woman who calls herself Kosmic plays sounds recombinant of android music fresh from Stockholm, Latex Lagoon reaches into his case of 240 hours of tapes and splays us with low static bass reverbs cut at the wavering boundaries of ecstasy and dread, and Scanner gives us a bonus track: an intense drone-like scan of big thunder voice sounds pitched downwards into infinity mixed with the soft sighs of phone sex. A "Sound Spore" of an evening with the Scanner crowd. The kind of scanner body wash where the skin peels off the face to reveal disintegrating flesh and skulls and brain tissue, arms are scanned into dead-air pixel imagery, and bodies arch upwards in bursts of high-energy sound waves as they evaporate into the Net.

Scanner is an assembler of the electronic past in our digital future. Forsaking improved vision, he provides us with improved hearing for detecting the sounds of our own disappearance into the electronic grid of dead space.

SONY FROM HELL

Dear cris,

Congrats on the Sony gold award. Reminds us of the time were were doing some work with the CEO of a hot-shot computer imaging company. When we described our work as "SONY from Hell," he got beet red in the face, slather began to spit out of his twisted lips, and he said: "You are never, never to say: 'SONY from Hell!" Like Bart Simpson, we immediately replied: "How are we going to speak about hell if we don't say hell? Hell, Hell, Hell, Sony, Sony, Sony! Needless to say, we were out of there immediately. But at least they had a limo waiting to drive us to the nearest border town.

A & M

****

Dear Arthur and Marilouise

Liked your Sony story a lot. There's a terrific graffiti on a black brick bridge leaving London for Heathrow Airport which reads:

For God So Loved His Only Begotten Son(y)

love
cris

W I R E D   S K I N

There's no difference between computer coding today and St. Augustine's writing De Trinitate at the end of the fourth century. They are both about putting out code, writing the aesthetic horizon for their times. Coders are the saints and potential heretics of digital reality.

MICROLASH

We once knew a group of coders in Seattle who were heavily into the SM scene. Every day they went from the high tech of digital coding to the low tech of whips, chains, and stiletto heels. During the daylight hours their minds might have been harvested by the virtual future, but at night their bodies were disciplined by simulations of dungeons, leather, and other nostalgia-ware from the virtual (bondage) past.

It's the very same in Toronto. Recently at one of those "Cybering Up" conferences for techno-business on the so-called information superhighway, we were struck by the composition of the audience. Not just your usual Silicon Valley khaki crowd, but a whole new digital fashion scene: women dressed in high black leather boots with stiletto razor-sharp metal heels, and guys with tight leather pants, bare and beautiful torsos, and dog collars with three-inch nails. We finally understood why we couldn't get to sleep at night because of the sounds of whips and chains and wet spanking leather coming from all the hotel rooms.

COMPUTER CODERS AS
21ST CENTURY MYSTICS

Could there be such fascination with SM today because computer coders and cyber-business missionaries are the first to feel the emotional effects of digital reality? The first, that is, to go psychically numb as they are harvested of their bodily feelings when their senses are externalized into image-based processing machines. Standing at the interface of the old 20th century body of flesh and bone and the new 21st century body of fibroblast cells and dark fiber skeletons, the leading edge of the new technological class cannot stand the strain of the externalization of the central nervous system. It panics and heads for the emotional intensity of SM. Starved for feeling in the cyber-factories of wired culture, digital flesh opts at the first opportunity for the dungeon. Or so the conventional theory goes.

Or maybe something very different. Perhaps digital coding and SM are flip sides of the same high-density body disk. Traditionally, the fascination of SM is that it is a ritualistic practice: codes of permission and transgression, an aesthetic ritual of pleasure that comes as much from the aesthetics of transgression as from the physical activity itself. Read the Marquis de Sade. Long before digital reality, SM played with the signs of the coded body. Pushing beyond the disciplining of the body, SM is all about the mysticism of the limit experience.

That's the very same as coding. Every coder worth her digital salt knows that the real creativity of coding lies not in the endless repetition of the same, just "doing code", but in those fabulous moments of folded space, when the code is transgressed and you finally break through to the n-dimension of the "cynical code." The cynical code? That's that mystical moment when you've been working for twenty hours straight, frustrated and angry and obsessive and determined more than ever. You hunker down at the flickering screen, put your digital mind on cool-line android frequency, and begin to program right at the speed edge of system codes and crash codes. Running the highwire act between boring, but functional, operating codes and the forbidden lure of no-go codes, you suddenly find yourself in that crash space where coding and decoding reverse fields and violently combine, folding back on one another, and you know, you just know, that you've broken through the dead-weight of the ritual of the code to that sweet telematic dreamland of outlaw codes, that floating space which Eastern mystics like to call virtual nothingness. It's not the code you want any longer or even the anti-code, but just that folded moment of virtual mysticism, when the aesthetic field reverses and repolarizes with a new digital horizon. And you've created it.

Like SM before it, computer coding is about the (virtual) limit experience. What's really going on in the dungeons at night is a fast reprise of coding during the day. What every coder searches for, and sometimes finds, in submission to their special dominatrix is a bodily expression of virtual mysticism: that thread of the doubled language of the body that will take them through to the folded space of the aesthetics of pleasure. Like a test pilot at the edge of the envelope, every digital coder always seeks the digital limit experience, and the limit experience is exactly what SM is all about. High tech learning labs, SM dungeons teach coders the tricks of the digital trade by inscribing on their bodies the hard lessons of the doubled sign of bodily pleasure and pain. Which is to say that SM has never been about pleasure and pain at all, but about delaying pleasure and introducing a tantalizing hint of uncertainty into the menu of pain. In this case, SM is not a way of breaking psychic numbness and feeling something again by beating feeling out of the body, but a way of intensifying numbness. Two rituals, then, of bodily estrangement. One to data, the other to the lash.

Stories for the Flesh-Eating 90s

Some like to call it the "Year of the Internet"
but we call it the year when the flesh-eating 90s
really got underway.

The Flesh-Eating 90s?

That's the body dried up, hardened, and flushed out under the
impact velocity of the will to purity.

These are our virtual road stories on contemporary culture. They
begin when life runs on empty, and in the gathering shadows
all that remains are memories of a future that's already in our
past. The millennial madness of '90s culture. They're called:
"Stories for the Flesh-Eating '90s." And we're not talking
about lettuce.

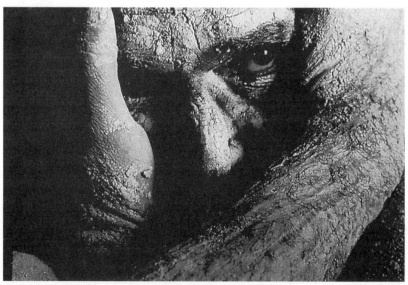

Paul Winternitz

DEAD DOGS AND DADDY UNDER
THE CHRISTMAS TREE

Merry Christmas

You can't go home again?
That's definitely not true
because at Christmas you can always only go home
And sometimes it's real grisly:
stories of arthritic eyes and black spots
and tumors and cancers and angina
and heart attacks
for the twelve very merry days of Christmas
or stories of my best friend Doug
who stabbed his Daddy to death
and left his body under the Christmas tree until March
with Rex, the good ole' family dog
Now Doug was schizoid, but so was his Daddy
so I guess it was only just a matter of time,
or circumstance,
to see which delusion won out:
Oedipus revenged
or Merry Christmas Dad From Hell.
Or I'm out shopping with my Mother,
buying her a spanking new Toshiba TV
with close-captioning and digital ports galore
for a happy multi-media future,
and she suddenly says:
"Did you see the manager of the store?

Well, a few weeks ago,
his wife went down to the highway
and threw herself in front of a transport truck.
Left three children. Sort of sad... I guess."
This was just after we drove by the house
of the family doctor,
the one who had acid thrown on his face
during a happy yuletide season past
by an unhappy patient hiding in the back of his car after
a housecall.
And it was just after our next door neighbour
of many years
said goodnight to his wife, had a last drink
with the boys down at the Legion
turned on all the lights in the house,
went into the basement
and blew his head off with a .410 double-barrelled
shotgun.
Three months later his oldest son,
with whom he never had good relations anyway
did the very same thing.
Drove his girlfriend to work,
getting out of the car
she said: "See you later."
He said: "Maybe"
And he was right
Because on the same day
he killed himself over his father's grave
Same gun, Different shells.

HAPPY NEW YEAR

It's New Year's Eve at the ballroom of the Hilton Hotel in downtown Montreal. The usual for a nostalgia-flavored party staged by the local oldies' radio station.

It could be a high school reunion or a one-night cruise on the Good Ship Lollipop. Nothing new, everything old except, of course, we're celebrating a New Year.

Everyone is dressed for the occasion with lots of shimmer and shine. But one outfit really does stand out. It's a woman wearing a sweater that spells out "Happy Holidays" in large battery-operated flashing neon letters.

And it's a big inspiration to us all, a kind of talisman taking us into the New Year. Fat guys begin to dance on tables, conga lines form and snake their way around the ballroom floor, empty champagne glasses are pyramided thirty high on tables filled with sparklers and red, blue and gold noisemakers, and the Pink Cadillacs get us to dance with their golden oldies' tunes, from Danny and the Juniors' **At the Hop** to Elvis' **Suspicious Minds** and Jerry Lee Lewis' **Great Balls of Fire.**

Of course, no one mentions that Danny slit his throat one night in a motel room, and left a note saying that he just couldn't stand singing that song one more time.

We all know what happened to Elvis.

And Jerry Lee Lewis? Well, **there is** all that talk about his dead wives.

A frightening ritual of fake ecstasy and real nostalgia.

HAPPY HOLIDAYS!

SHOPPING FOR JESUS

It's Easter Sunday in Montreal
And I'm doing my very best for baby Jesus
Dragging a pixel cross through the streets of the old city
on a pilgrimage to the Oratory
high on the hill.
Yeah, the one with Brother Andre's heart
on grisly display.
Rumor has it the heart went missing in '65
Stolen by the mob
and held for ransom,
But the Church just said:
"Keep it. There's plenty more where that came from."

And it's a truly swell parade
Seems that just everyone has come out for the big party
of death and resurrection,
Elvis look-alikes
Cross-dressing Madonnas
the restless, drifting soul of Kurt Cobain
and I swear that just ahead of me
Princess Di and Jackie O are all dressed up in
their Easter Sunday finery

A woman on stilts walks across the way
carrying the head of John the Baptist
on a plate to Planet Hollywood

The tomb is empty
Maybe it's waiting for us

And the cross is penance
"Sure, and I'm a natural born virgin,"
Madonna whispers in my ear.

Will Bauer, Steve Gibson, Raonull Conover

SLASH AND BURN

We're sitting in a cyber-coffee bar in San Francisco talking to Denise. A dancer by night and an artist by day, Denise is strikingly beautiful in a delicate, porcelain-like way: tall, slim with shoulder-length auburn hair, pierced nose, lip, and, of course, a single eyebrow. At one point she stood up, turned with her back towards us, displaying magnificent tattoos in the form of multi-color angel wings that went from her shoulder-blades down to the small of her back in the colors of the most exquisite medieval stained-glass, and all this cut by slender red scars splayed up and down her arms.

We ask about the scars and she tells us about the latest SM scene in the City. It seems these days that in the hip areas of San Francisco the body cybernetic is out-of-date, unplugged from outlaw consciousness and allowed to float off into the East where the tech-hype is only now getting underway. What's really new in SF these days is some pain cut with a lot of healing. It's called Slash and Burn. Cut long slits down your arms or legs, really any flesh will do, pour a bit of gasoline into the wounds, and then ignite the flesh. Now, don't let it burn too long, we're not talking about flesh arson here, about burning down the whole barn of the body in a massive end-of-the-century conflagration, but about pain with a recuperative purpose. As Denise explains: the real joy of inflicting pain on your own body lies in the pleasure of the healing process. It's almost addictive. Cut the flesh, pour on gas, watch it burn, and then eagerly anticipate the long, slow healing powers of the body.

The body in San Francisco, then, as all about cynical feelings intensifying the pain of the flesh to get one last hit of the angel wings of bodily healing.

BRANDED FLESH

Who says the American frontier
with its vision tough and nostalgic
of the Old West
has gone terminal?
A friend calls from Los Angeles
to say
that branding flesh
on California college campuses
is all the rage these days.
Not just ordinary branding
with tattoos:
That's passe and artsy and territorial
and no one cares about that anymore
but sign-branding,
that point where consumer brands
finally fly off
all the T-shirts, hats, and jeans on
city streets
and get welded onto the poker end
of good-old fashion cattle branders:
CK, M for MacDonalds, Wranglers
heated up liquid red in open flames
and then four at a time
are burnt on flesh
of waiting bodies
"It melts flesh like butter"

Leif Harmsen

72

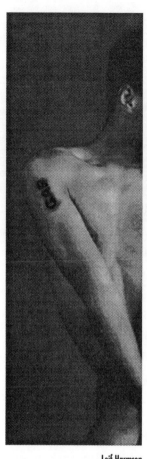

one branding wrangler was heard
to say
in approving, but awed, tones
And, of course, the usual:
The very next day
California college administrators
passed a new edict
forbidding in the future
"open fires" on campus.

Leif Harmsen

73

"BRAINS LIVE A LITTLE BIT LONGER"

Paul Winternitz

I had a dream last night about my Dad. He died in '67, and I've never not thought about him. Probably because I never had the chance to say goodbye. And it was strange. I walk into an empty room, except for a closed coffin. I pry open the lid, and my Dad, really none the worse for wear, opens his eyes, sits up in the coffin, and we start talking about everyday things. There are autopsy cuts on his body, and his ears are still deep blue from the stroke, but he climbs out of the casket and it's like old times again. Except I have this feeling that things aren't just right, that he's dead now, and this is going to end, that maybe it should never have happened. I think my Dad gets the drift of my dream-thoughts, because he suddenly turns to me and says: "Hey Art, the body dies, but sometimes the brain lives a little bit longer."

CODE WARRIORS

BUNKERING IN AND DUMBING DOWN

Electronic technology terminates with the radically divided self: the self, that is, which is at war with itself. Split consciousness for a culture that is split between digital- and human flesh.

A warring field, the electronic self is torn between contradictory impulses towards privacy and the public, the natural self and the social self, private imagination and electronic fantasy. The price for reconciling the divided self by sacrificing one side of the electronic personality is severe. If it abandons private identity and actually *becomes media* (Cineplex mind, IMAX imagination, MTV chat, CNN nerves), the electronic self will suffer terminal repression. However, if it seals itself off from public life by retreating to an electronic cell in the suburbs or a computer condo in the city, it quickly falls into an irreal world of electronic MOO-room fun within the armoured windows. Suffering electronic amnesia on the public and its multiple viewpoints, going private means that the electronic self will not be in a position to maximize its interests by struggling in an increasingly competitive economic field.

The electronic self is in a bind. Seeking to immunize itself against the worst effects of public life, it bunkers in. It becomes a pure will-for-itself: self-dwelling, closed down, ready to sacrifice all other interests for the sake of its own immunity. Bunkering in is the epochal consciousness of technological society in its most mature phase. McLuhan called it the "cool personality" typical of the TV age, others have spoken of "cocooning" away the 90s, but we would say that bunkering in is about something really simple: being sick of others and trying to shelter the beleagured self in a techno-bubble. Dipping back to Darwin, West Coast libertarians like to talk today about "survival of the electronically fittest."

However, at the same time that the electronic self bunkers in as a survival strategy, it is forced out of economic necessity to stick its head out of its techno-bubble and skate to work. Frightened by the accelerating speed of technological change, distressed by the loss of disposable income, worried about a future without jobs, and angry at the government, the electronic self oscillates between fear and rage. Rather than objectify its anger in a critical analysis of the public situation, diagnosing, for example, the deep relationship between the rise of the technological class and the loss of jobs, the electronic self is taught by the media elite to turn the "self" into a form of self-contempt. Dumbing down becomes the reality of the late 20th century personality. Dumbing down? In its benign form, that's Gump with his box of chocolates and Homer Simpson barfing doughnuts. In its predatory form, it's everyday life: cons and parasites and computer presidents and killer Jeeps on city streets. Or, like in *Pulp Fiction,* maybe it's time to "bring out the gimp."

The bunker self is infected by ressentiment against those it holds responsible for what ails it (feminists, African-Americans, immigrants, single mothers on welfare); dumbing down is the last blast of slave consciousness (servile to authority; abusive to those weaker than it). Petulant and given over to bouts of whining about the petty inconveniences, bunkering in knows no ethics other than immediate self-gratification. Hard-eyed and emotionally cryogenicized, dumbing down means oscillating between the psychological poles of predator and clown. Between the illusion of immunity and the reality of the process-self, that's the radically divided state of the electronic personality at the end of the 20th century. Just in time to catch the virtual screen opening up on the final file of the millennium, the bunker ego and the dumbed down self are the culmination of what Jean-Paul Sartre predicted: a schizoid self which is simultaneously in-itself and for-itself, an unreconciled self flipping between illusion and self-contempt. Today, it's hip to be dumb, and smart to be turned off and tuned out.

The psychological war zone of bunkering in and dumbing down is the actual cultural context out of which emerges technological euphoria. Digital reality is perfect. It provides the bunker self with immediate, universal access to a global community *without people*: electronic communication without social contact, being digital without being human, going on-line without leaving the safety of the electronic bunker. The bunker self takes to the Internet like a pixel to a screen because the information superhighway is the biggest theme park in the world: more than 170 countries. And it's perfect too for dumbing down. Privileging information while exterminating meaning, surfing without engagement, digital reality provides a new virtual playing-field for tuning out and turning off. For example, when CITY-TV (Toronto) recently announced a merger with Voyager to produce new multi-media productions, its first product of choice was the creation of an "electronic rumpus room." Playtime for the new electronic kids on the block.

What's better, with the quick privatization of the Internet and the Web, the predatory self doesn't have to risk brief dashes in and out of public life to grab what it wants. In virtual capitalism, the predatory self goes fully digital, arms itself with the latest in graphical interfaces, bulks up the profile of its homepage, and goes hunting for digital gold. Schumpeter might have talked about "creative destruction" as the contemporary phase of transiting to a virtual economy, but the predatory self knows better. Turbulence in the field means one thing only: the rest position is terminal, victory goes to those who warp jump the fastest to cyberspace. Working on the tried but true formula of "use and abandon," the predatory self does the ultimate dumbing-down trick: it sheds its flesh (for cyber-skin), its mind (for distributive intelligence), its nerves (for algorithmic codes), its sex organs (for digital seduction), its limbs (for virtual vectors of speed and slipstream access), and its history (for multiplex hard ram). Virtual Gump.

OPENING OUT AND SMARTENING UP

Two Worlds

Digital reality contains alternative possibilities towards emancipation and domination.

As a manifestation of the power of the virtual class, digital reality has definitely plunged the world into a great historical crisis. Here cybertechnology is a grisly process of harvesting nature and culture, and particularly our bodies, for fast-rendering through massive virtual imaging-systems. Not a technology that we can hold outside of ourselves as an inanimate object, cybertechnology has actually come alive in the form of virtualization. It seeks to take possession of the material world, and to dump material reality into the electronic trashbin in favor of what has been eloquently described as a "realm inhabitated by the disembodied." Cybertechnology creates two worlds, one virtual, the other material, separate and unequal. The radical division between these two worlds is becoming more apparent every day.

The struggle to relink technology and ethics, to *think* cybertechnology in terms of the relationship of virtuality to questions of democracy, justice, social solidarity, and creative inquiry promises a path of reconciliation. Of course, we don't think of the body or nature as outside technology, but as part of a field of dynamic and often deeply conflicting relations in which, for example, the body itself could be construed as a "technology." This being so, the key ethical question might be: what are the possibilities for a virtual democracy, virtual justice, virtual solidarity, and virtual knowledge? Rather than recover ethics outside of cybertechnology, our position is to force ethics to travel deeply and quickly inside the force-field of cybertechnology, to make our ethical demands for social justice, for the reconciliation of flesh and spirit, rub up against the most demonic aspects of virtual reality. In this we practice Foucault's prescription for reading Nietzsche, that honors a writer (or a new ethics) by forcing ethics to bend, crackle, strain, and groan under the violence and weight of our insistent demands for meaning.

Post-Bodies

We are living in a decisive historical time: the era of the post-human. This age is typified by a relentless effort on the part of the virtual class to force a wholesale abandonment of the body, to dump sensuous experience into the trashbin, substituting instead a disembodied world of empty data flows. This body assault takes different forms: from the rhetoric of the "information superhighway" (of which we are the pavement) to the widely publicized effort by Microsoft and McCaw Cellular to develop a global multi-media network of satellites for downloading and uplinking the archival record of the human experience into massive, centrally controlled data bases. The virtual elite always present the "electronic frontier" in the glowing, ideological terms of heightened accessibility, increased (cyber-knowledge), more "rapid delivery of health and education to rural environments" or better paying high-tech jobs. In reality what they are doing is delivering us to virtualization.

It isn't a matter of being pro- or anti-technology, but of considering the consequences of virtual reality when it is so deeply spoken of in the language of exterminism. In the age of the virtual class, digital technology works to discredit bodily experience, to make us feel humiliated and inferior to the virtual rendering of the body in its different electronic formats, from computers and television to the glitzy and vampirish world of advertising. The attitude that the body is a failed project takes us directly to a culture driven by suicidal nihilism. Remember Goya: imagination without reason begets monstrous visions. Those "monstrous visions" are the designs for better electronic bodies that vomit out of the cyber-factories of the Silicon Valleys of the world every day.

Digital reality has given us artificial life. Not artificial life as an abstract telematic experience fabricated by techno-labs, but artificial life as life as it is actually lived today. Cybertechnology has escaped the digital labs, and has inscribed itself on our captive bodies. In artificial life, the body is a violent uncertainty-field. What could be spoken of in the 1930s only in the language of high-energy physics, particularly Heisenberg's concept of uncertainty, has now been materialized in society as the schizoid body: the body, that is, as an unstable field flipping aimlessly between opposing poles: bunkered in yet dumbed down. This is the symptomic sign of what we call the digital body.

The New Power Elite

There are two dominant political tendencies in the 1990s: a global "virtual class" that presents the *particular* interests of technotopia as the *general* human interest, and the equally swift emergence of ever more grisly forms of conservative fundamentalism in response to the hegemony of the virtual class.

The virtual class is composed of monarchs of the electronic kingdom. Its members like to gather in digital nests, from Silicon Valley and Chiba City to the European cyber-grid running from Munich to Grenoble. Deeply authoritarian in its politics, it seeks to exclude from public debate any perspective that challenges the ruling ideology of technotopia. Like its historical predecessors, the early bourgeoisie of primitive capitalism, the virtual class is driven by the belief that a cybernetically-steered society, of which it is the guiding helmsman, is coeval with the noblest aspirations of human destiny. Listen to the rhetoric of the virtual class that drowns the mediascape. A few years ago, at Silicon Graphics, Clinton preached the technotopian gospel that the "information superhighway" is the telematic destiny of America; Gore continues to hype the "interactive society" as the next stage of human evolution; Microsoft presents its strategic plans for a world wide web of digital satellites in the soft language of doing a big service for humanity (William Gates said his new satellite system would allow educational and health services to be delivered to previously inaccessible rural areas); and all multinational business and most governments these days commonly chant the refrain that trade policy should be decoupled from human rights issues. For example, faced with American business opposition to his executive order linking China's "Most Favored Nation" status to improvements in human rights, Clinton instantly collapsed, announcing that he had "deep regrets" about his own executive order. Of course, in the mid-90s the gospel of technotopia is the bible of virtual libertarians, Newt Gingrich most of all.

While the ruling masters of the virtual class in countries ranging from the United States, Japan, Western Europe and Canada represent the territorial centre of digital power, the rest of the world is quickly remaindered. Based in labor that is not a fungible resource, the middle- and working classes in all countries are repeatedly victimized by the virtual class. Today, labor is disciplined by the representatives of the virtual class who occupy the highest policy-making positions of government. As the dominant ideology of the 90s, the virtual class institutes draconian anti-labor policies mandating "labor adjustment," "free trade," and belt-tightening, and all of this backed up by a media mantra calling for global economic competition, an end to pay equity, and for a "meaner and leaner" workplace.

For those outside the labor force—the jobless, the disenfranchised, the politically powerless, the surplus class—the disciplinary lessons administered by the virtual class are bitter. And it fits so perfectly with the psychology of bunkering in. Consider the silence at the terrorism in Haiti where in a macabre replay of Machiavelli's strategies for stable political rule, the tortured bodies of political activists had their faces cut off, were thrown into the main streets of Port-au-Prince, and left there under the glaring sun for several days. The police did not allow anyone to take away the bodies. Pigs ate the rotting flesh. The lesson is clear: the state has all-pervasive power to the point that even the identities of its victims after death can be effaced, letting the spirits of the dead roam in endless anguish. This is diabolical power at the end of the twentieth-century, and still not a humanitarian peep from the political managers of the virtual class. Not until the shores of America were filled with "illegal" Haitian refugees did the Clinton Administration react. Or consider the moral culpability of the so-called "creative leadership" of the virtual societies of the West who continue to turn a blinkered eye to the genocide that takes place in the streets of Sarajevo everyday. Would it be different if Bosnia had oil, a Nike running shoe factory, or, even better, a Microsoft chip mill?

The virtual elite has the ethics of the hangman, all hidden under the soft hype of the data superhighway as new body wetware for the twenty-first century.

Dominant Ideology

Recently, we received the following letter from Nate McFadden, a free-lance reporter for a San Francisco magazine:

> In the *SF Bay Guardian's* article on *Wired*, a former director of The Well, Cliff Figallo, commented on the colonization of cyberspace. "To some of us, it's like the staking of claims in the Old West. Perhaps it's the manifest destiny of cyberspace."
>
> This remark seems to verify, at least a little, the lack of moral awareness rampant in the techno-elite. For me, the apparently unironic usage of the expression "manifest destiny" indicates a mindset that avoids historical antecedents, and is free from any critical examination of motive and result.

A little later, we received this email message from Mark Schneider, Vancouver bureau chief for CTV:

> Check out the latest issue of *The Nation* (July 3), "Whose Net Is It?" by Andrew Shapiro.
>
> "You probably didn't notice, but the Internet was sold a few months ago. Well, sort of: The Federal government has been gradually transferring the backbone of the US portion of the global computer network to companies such as IBM and MCI as part of a larger plan to privatize cyberspace. But the crucial step was taken on April 30, when the National Science Foundation shut down its part of the Internet... [that's left] the corporate giants in charge..."

The virtual elite is a mixture of predatory capitalists and vision-ary computer specialists for whom virtualization is about our disappearance into nothingness. We are talking about a system-atic assault against the human species, a virtual war strategy where knowledge is reduced to data storage dumps, friendship is dissolved into floating cyber-interactions, and communication means the end of meaning. Virtualization in the cyber-hands of the new technological class is all about *our* being dumbed down. In a very practical way, the end of the 20th century is characterized by the laying down of hardware (virtual railway tracks) across the ever-expanding electronic frontier. Of course, who controls the hardware will dominate the soft(ware) cul-ture of the 21st century. That's why Microsoft is the first of all the 21st century corporations: it's already put the Operating System in place and now, through Microsoft Network, it's set to actually *be* the Internet.

All of this is being done without any substantive public debate, to the background tune, in fact, of three cheers for the virtual home team and its hyped-ideology of cybertechnology as emancipation. Manifest Destiny has come inside (us), and we are the once and future victims of the big (electronic) stick.

Manifest (Virtual) Destiny

The resuscitation of the doctrine of Manifest Destiny as the bi-ble of the virtual class has already taken place. However, it's no longer Manifest Destiny as an American war strategy for the endocolonization of North America, but a more vicious doctrine of digital inevitability that is being put in place around the globe by the technological elite. In this mutation of Manifest Destiny, the world is quickly divided into privileged virtual economies, passive storage depots for cheap labor, and permanently slaved-nations. While the citizens of the lead virtual societies certainly suffer massive psychological repression and suppression (of so-cial choices), countries which are patched into the political economy of virtual reality as sources of cheap manufacturing or as product assembly labor suffer the form of domination par-ticular to primitive capitalism—"work or starve." For the citizens of the slaved-nations, from Africa to Haiti, they are sim-ply put under the coercive welfare wardship of a newly militant United Nations and then erased from historical consciousness. Like all empires before it, virtual reality begins with a blood-sac-rifice.

Contradictions of the Virtual Class

It is not at all clear that the new technological class will win the day. The will to virtuality is riddled with deep contradictions. Can the offensive by the virtual class against human labor actu-ally succeed in light of both growing impoverishment and the crushing of life expectations for the young? The rhetoric of dig-ital reality speaks about the growing abundance of high-paying jobs in the tech industry. Across the OECD, the reality is dra-matically different: every country that has instituted policies promoting the expansion of digital reality has witnessed a dra-matic, and seemingly permanent, increase in unemployment. Joblessness not just in the low- or no tech industries, but mas-sive layoffs and ruthless "restructurings" in the vaunted digital industries themselves. No one bothered to tell us that digital re-ality also deletes jobs! This is the dirty little secret that the masters of the technological universe definitely don't want to talk about, and in their control of the mediascape will never al-low to be spoken. It's the forbidden-to-be-thought truth that ruptures the seamless web of digital reality as the dominant ide-ology of the 90s.

Can the offensive by the technological class against society in the name of the moral superiority of digital reality be sustained in the midst of a general social crisis that it has created? What will happen when digital reality, this dynamic drive to planetary mastery in the name of technology, actually begins to displace its creators— the virtual class?

Against the new technological class are ranged a series of critical political forces: Net knowledgeable, technically astute, people who speak on behalf of the new relations of digital reality rather than apologizing for the old forces of commercial or governmental interests. Certainly Net surfers with a (critical) attitude who attempt to make the "information superhighway" serve the ethical human ends of solidarity, creativity, and democracy, but also all of those social movements who both say 'no' to the virtual class, and 'yes' to rethinking the human destiny. We have in mind aboriginal movements from North and South America who make of the issue of land rights a fundamental battleground of (durational) time against (virtualized) space, feminists who have reasserted the identity of the body, the Green movement which is slowly turning the tide on a global scale against the harvesting machine of corporate capitalism, and those "body outlaws," bisexuals and gays and lesbians, who have made of the politics of sexual difference a way of speaking again about the possibility of human love.

Having said this, we are under no illusion about the fundamental exterminatory character of the times. We exist now at a great divide: between a fall into a new form of despotic capitalism on the one hand, and a world that might be recreated ethically on the other. This is the life-and-death struggle of our age.

Harvesting Flesh

Contemporary culture is driven onwards by the planetary drive towards the mastery of nature. In Heidegger's chilling description, technology is infected with the language of "harvesting." First, the harvesting of nature as the physical world is reduced to a passive resource of exploitation. And second, the harvesting of human flesh as (our) bodies and minds are reduced to a data base for imaging systems. That's the contemporary human fate: to be dumped into the waiting data archives for purposes of future resequencing. Some all Web brains, others TV heads or designer logos, here minds as media screens, there nerves as electronic impulses finely tuned to the rhythms of the digital world.

Consider TV: a war machine for colonizing the soft mass of the electronic mind. Three tactical manoeuvres are always in play: *Desensitization* —following exactly the same procedure used by the C.I.A. in training assassins, TV desensitizes the electronic mind by repeatedly exposing it to scenes of torture, corpses, and mutilation. By reducing the electronic mind of the population to the deadened morality of the assassin, it preps the population for its own future sacrifice in the form of body dumps; *Infantilization* —that's the gradual media strategy for reducing us all to retro-children: perfect political fodder for the growth of virtual- and retro-fascism); and *Reenergization* —left to its own devices, the mediascape will always collapse towards its inertial pole. That's why the media must constantly be reenergized (recharged?) by scenes of sacrificial violence. In every war, there are victims and executioners. In the television war machine, we are always *both*: victims (of the three tactical maneouvres of the mediscape), and executioners of an accidental range of victims dragged across the cold screens for our moral dismissal (much like the terminal judgement of the

Roman masses in the amphitheatres of classical antiquity).

Photography, cinema, TV, and the Internet are successive stages in virtualization. Beginning with the simulacrum of the first photograph, continuing with the scanner imaging-system of TV, and concluding (for the moment) with the data archives of the Internet, human experience is fast-dumped into the relays and networks of virtual culture. McLuhan was wrong. It is not the technological media of communication as an extension of man; but the human species as a humiliated subject of digital culture.

VIRTUAL ROAD STORIES

Warren Padula

SLUMMING IN GOPHER SPACE

Leif Harmsen emails from London to ask if we've gone slumming in gopher space. Seems that since the development of Netscape, the gopher has been abandoned and, like a telematic post-cursor of those empty American inner cities before it, everyone rushes out to the suburbs of the Web with its homepages plunked down on green biologic lawns like coast-to-coast Century 21 "For Sale" signs.

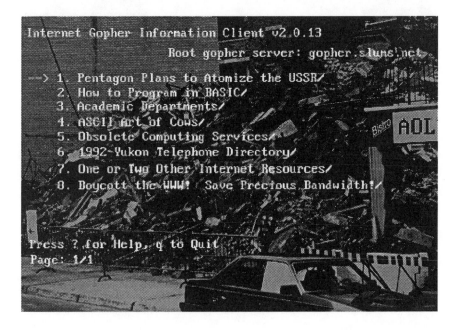

```
Internet Gopher Information Client v2.0.13
                    Root gopher server: gopher.slums.net

--> 1. Pentagon Plans to Atomize the USSR/
     2. How to Program in BASIC/
     3. Academic Departments/
     4. ASCII Art of Cows/
     5. Obsolete Computing Services/
     6. 1992 Yukon Telephone Directory/
     7. One or Two Other Internet Resources/
     8. Boycott the WWW! Save Precious Bandwidth!/




Press ? for Help, q to Quit
Page: 1/1
```

I never liked Gopher much anyway, too passive and archival and information-serious, but I check it out, and it's true. You float down empty pixel hallways of data circa 1993, tomes sometimes fall off unattended shelves, the turnstiles are covered with guck from gallium arsenate in its decaying stage, the registration desk stands empty with signs everywhere of hasty flight, and whirpool storms of dust balls swirl through the digital air. Sort of like the Texas panhandle after the tornado, when you peek your head out of the basement, squinting at the Day of the Living Dead sunlight, the land is empty from horizon to horizon, and you just don't know whether you're at the end of all things or the beginning again and again of the big rebuilding. Vectoring through the vacant storage vaults of the Gopher, no one is around, you can hear your voice echo as it lazily accelerates its sonic way through the matrix, but like a good cyber-citizen who wants to stay alive for one last go-round on the mall strips of the Web, you wear your hard hat as protection against falling data beams.

I'm outta here.

FROM SILICON ILLUSIONS TO DESERT DREAMLANDS

We're on a plane from LAX to the McCarran International Airport in Las Vegas. Just that morning we exited the tech-hype of Silicon Valley, taking one last ride with the nomadic travellers of the information superhighway from San Francisco to Los Angeles. Clean-cut coastie computer flesh on a fast roll from the artificial intelligence labs of the Valley to the virtual reality entertainment centres of Hollywood. Designers for the twenty-first century body bringing down secret algorithmic codes for newer and better image-capturing systems for fast-diffusion through the American psyche via the cultural galaxy of Hollywood. At Los Angeles, the computer crowd transited the commuter jet and their body vectors were immediately replaced by a fun crowd, some for a weekend special of gambling and the shows just getting out of their daily life, others with cold smiles and flashy clothes, hard-drinking, hard-living, high-rolling gambling faces. Like the two big guys who sat in front of us, who could have been high-rollers or no-rollers, but who were definitely there for the game. They were beautiful in the way only the slick-ass mean streets crowd can be. They talked quietly about the money they were carrying for the tables (not much), and how they've got this "blonde babe" who just might be prevailed upon to put them up for a few nights. And then there was the fight crowd with shoulders almost as wide as the plane and gold jewellery heavy enough to have to be tagged as extra baggage. The techies might have had tight sphincters about the future virtual, but the Las Vegas crowd rode a tension edge, just between giddy anticipation of the games of seduction to come and real life knowledge of their (lowly) place in the table of power. They knew where they were going: dressed for Las Vegas success.

GOODBYE TECHNORAMA. HELLO DESERT DREAMLANDS.

Leif Harmsen

TREASURE ISLAND AT THE MIRAGE

USAIR flight #1904 banks over the Luxor resort and triangulates on the Roaring Lion of the MGM Grand, the Exploding Volcano (on a closed 15-minute loop) at the Mirage, and the just dynamited remains of the Dunes as it completes the hump from LAX to the City of Broken Dreams.

As soon as the plane stops rolling, the captain comes down the aisle, exchanging dollar bills for what look like popcorn containers filled with quarters. And just in time, too! Because before the body hits the bleached streets with that parched noon-day sun, before the skin is grilled by summer heat that just makes you loco like a fire that burns without consuming, well before all of that, you're flipped into the super-chilled air-conditioning of the airport lounge with its gleaming silver trimmings and dead-air palm trees, and your ears go cyber at the roar of the bells and whistles and clanging and whirring from all multi-tasked banks of slot machines, Las Vegas style. So you play ten bucks, win a few of the lever-pulls, but like a chicken in a Skinner box you're under the fatal spell of losing everything in an S/R game that you don't understand, so you get your luggage and head straight for the taxi stand.

The ride into the Strip was everything you could of hoped for. All the taxis were taken, except for an old mini-bus. "Five dollars a head," the driver shills, but he forgets to add "with a lot of abuse." So we're driving from the airport to our hotel, the Treasure Island at the Mirage. We've read the tourist brochure which describes in exotic and mouth-watering detail the $450 million dollar "Pirate Theme Hotel" which includes hourly sea battles between two ninety-foot replicas of 18th century sailing ships. The driver asks the address, instantly sizes us up and takes his first body shot: "The Mirage or Treasure Island? They're two different hotels. Which one?" When I answer, "Treasure Island at the Mirage," he says: "Oh! The small one." (the brochure had bragged about it as being the "seventh largest hotel in the world with 2,900 rooms"). And yet he laughs: "That's just a gimmick. The Treasure Island is NOT the Mirage." I already feel defensive about a hotel I thought I didn't care about in a city I've never visited.

The minibus ride is a perfect scene out of the **Day of the Locusts**, that's the name I've given to the driver who has decided to make us his sacrificial victims for the day. We're dressed in regulation black, the color of suspicion to Las Vegas eyes. Sitting next to us is a couple in their mid-forties who say they are from St. Louis and just out for a good time on the Strip. Actually, the guy is next to us and the woman is sitting on his lap, a blue skirt riding high over her thighs. She's also got on a tight white blouse, a gold chain with a rhinestone pendant, and has a Bloody Mary in her hand. I notice her outfit when she suddenly announces: "I've **really** got to pee!" She offers Day of the Locusts a piece of celery. "Vegetables are good for you," she coos.

He jokes right back. "Did you hear the one about the man married to the woman who was hard-of-hearing. She had eighteen children. Every night when they went to bed, he'd say to her: 'Do you want to go to sleep or what?' She'd strain to hear, cup her ear and answer: 'What?'" Day of the Locusts and the couple from St. Louis have a good chuckle about that.

We remain silent, perfect marks for the sacrifice. They've already united in a complicit understanding of how things really work: a kind of fleshy, raw notion of life as it's actually lived.

We turn the corner, and there's a sign for the University of Nevada. They all laugh. The driver says: "If it wasn't for the **Running Rebels**, I'd never know there was a University there." They all laugh again.

We know they've got us.

LAS VEGAS THEME PARK

Warren Padula

Las Vegas is America
at the 3d millennium
A theme park
of hope and desolation
where prophets of the Old Testament
Job most of all,
sometimes give up the ghost,
walk out of the desert
and take their noon-day place
at the blackjack tables

Along the boulevard of broken dreams
the dusty, windy gutters are filled
with crumbling flyers
for sex
Las Vegas style

Just outside of Caesar's Palace
gamblers on bended knees
make offerings of incense and prayer
at the shrine of the American Buddha
under the desert sun

Not Babylon revisited
but a hybrid Babylon for a hybrid America
showgirls and dying elephants
and white tigers and Cirque de Soleil
and hot air and cold air to the hyper
and total surveillance
and gamblers and hustlers
and losers and winners
and junior moms and dads with strap-on
baby pouches
come to the future
come to the theme park
come to pray one last time
all day and all night
at America's last and best mall
of magic and despair

THE CLAM KING

M. Kroker

Just off Highway # 3
the old road, sometimes called the Nashua Turnpike,
running between New Hamphire and Boston,
Not Interstate 93
with its big six lanes of crash car traffic
moving at hyper-velocity
taking the dormer communities
into the Boston office towers
with their little speckled dreams of
"Dress Down Fridays"
but Highway No. 3 as what passes for a
rural route in America these days,
tired and hungry and speed-crazy
you park your body in the Clam King.
Been doing this for ten years, every six or seven months
It's across the street from a fantastic
used-car Corvette dealership,
right across the way from empty textile factories

lining the Manchester River,
and very best of all,
just down the road from
bargain-basement clothes at Marshalls
and heart of the heart
country books at the Caldor's display:
It was in Caldor's one day
that I first spotted Kenneth Anger's
Hollywood Babylon,
the kind of book that is so good
that you don't want to buy it
because anything this delicious must be out of bounds,
not really serious just because it's really serious.
So, you leave Caldor's without the book
but every time you pass by that way again
your car suddenly goes on auto-pilot
and does a quick entry into the parking lot
so that your brain sickness
can be fed images of Dead Babylon
And it gets to be a habit:
Take Highway #3 to the Clam King
order a heaping plate of fried clams
(or little clamettes if you're not too hungry),
sit down with all the working clam-folks
from the surrounding towns
gaze out at the gleaming corvettes
each with a story to tell
about some mystery of the highway not yet explored,
listen to the lonely sounds of the cars sliding on by,

and read **Hollywood Babylon** again and again:
James Dean: the "human ashtray"
Jayne Mansfield: decapitated in a car accident
Marilyn Monroe: suicided
Charlie Chaplin: Hollywood's most famous chickenhawk
Drug overdoses, hotel fires,
murders of the stars by gun, by knife,
by strangulation, by love
All of the speed and violence and desire gone empty
of crash America is in **Hollywood Babylon,**
a kind of raw primitive truth
or maybe an illusion that's willed into truth
that you just know you want to feel
this dark hole of energy in its last sacrificial rites
to finally know America by its clam kings gone bust.

M. Kroker

SHOPPING THE SKY
MAJORICA PEARLS AT 5 MILES UP

Maybe it's because you're singled out
as the duty-free body zooming along
at escape velocity five miles up in high-rad space
with that waiting cart in the aisle
and the impatient stewardess:
Should you buy those Majorica pearls?

You're out in the neutral tax-free sky
your body has achieved lift-off
from the history of the waiting terminals
but you're bored and stuffed
and can't get enough oxygen
and the seat ahead of you is jammed tight
right up to your belly
and they keep feeding you soft food
to slow down excremental habits to inertia
and all the orifices, everyone
are plugged into happy electronic prosthetics
so that the duty-free body is cocooned
into a perfect comfort-zone,
into a perfect surveillance zone for crowd management
like Disneyland where your holiday job is to shut down
your body functions to minimal living requirements
like a bear in hibernation
or a turtle on a 300 year life cycle
you're zoned away

from yourself: technologies of entertainment
and most of all from the dreams forbidden
of the crash that never happens
but that's shopping in the sky for the body processed
and you still have those Majorica pearls on your mind
and it's embarrassing
because you know what's happening
first the stuffing up of the eyes:
movies edited for the airplaned body
then the plugging up of the ears:
hyper-treble rock 'n roll
the force-feeding of the stomach:
"Will that be chicken or beef?"
and now the cocooning of the body bored and restless:
shopping in the sky .
as the perfect model of consumption
maybe the last appearance of the mall
as it rockets its way into the high-trajectory orbit
of managed satisfactions
like those cigarettes
which you can no longer smoke in the sky
but there's still those Majorica pearls
and it's three hours from termination

LUMINOUS LUXOR LAS VEGAS

Warren Padula

The Luxor Hotel
with its pyramid shape, Egyptian motif
and brilliant light shining straight up into space,
is billed as "the 8th Wonder of the world".
And well it should!
With the Great Wall of China,
the Luxor is the only man-made earth object
that can be seen from deep space.
In fact, astronauts use it as a night light
for reading newspapers at ten miles up.
But maybe the Luxor really is
the 1st Wonder of the extra-terrestrial world
the very first ad for planet earth
that will be sighted by aliens, every one.

HACKING UFO'S IN
YUMA, ARIZONA

Saturday night and the digital dreamers download their drifting bodies at Andrew's place. Hacker musicians, multimedia programmers for Microsomething, nomad flesh just out for the night: all come together for beer and talk, cut with a lot of scotch and cigars.

Joe is just back from a road trip to Arizona. That great kind of mythic drive where you fly your body to Phoenix, rent a car, and head straight out across the desert flatlands to a magical hideaway in Sonora State, the ancestral home of the disappeared, ancient people in northern Mexico. He should have looked better, but he's nervous and tight strung and when asked by Flip, his all-season boyfriend, he tells us he's got a video to show us. OK. We all do the troop to the TV altar, flatass our bodies into recliner positions, and watch the first pixels of the video coming across the big blue screen. And it's great. It's a hard-driving car scene across the Arizona desert at dusk. The car stereo is turned loud to the rockin' sounds of Crash and background road trip chatter: the latest from **X Files**, fast-track lines from **The Simpsons**, an argument about what's best in new German electronic music: **Micro Dub Infection** or **Isolationism.** The kind of argument where there are no winners or losers, because who really cares in the end. A group of friends are doing the classic American road trip through Arizona desert country on a beautiful spring evening, Crash is acid-lined into your electronic ears, and you pitch your voice at just that right theoretical level, where everyone gets to do a elegant riff on the latest fads in the Berlin and London electronic music scenes, sort of a culture chat-line without the Net for hacking away the driving hours.

Shot from the backseat, the camcorder is capturing it all,

zooms, establishing shots, framing shots, perfect fades from front-seat head to chattering head. Suddenly, the video peeks out the windshield at the passing scenery, and there right before its video eyes are two gigantic luminous disks, actually more like telematic moons, in the sky. Our first UFO sighting. The voice recorder explodes with theories: Carl, the driver, starts waxing conspiratorially about how he's heard (from the **X-Files**) that they've got refrigerator cars full of aliens stored in the desert, Anna says that she knows there's a military base nearby, maybe it's secret new military aircraft (disguised to look like enormous silver moons in the evening sky) or false mirrors or phantom weather balloons. Instead of stopping to admire the alien scene, Carl, probably thinking about all those alien butt probers he's heard so much about, presses the pedal to the floor and rock 'n rolls the car to its pitch velocity.

And it seems to work. After 5 minutes or so, the UFO's disappear. Everybody relaxes, there's a lot of laughter and ears drift back to the sounds of Crash and to stories fabulous about aliens and UFO's and conspiracies and sightings. It's obvious that no one wants to take on the heavy historical burden of a UFO sighting, and that even with all the skepticism no one certainly wanted to take a chance of being abducted. Dreams forbidden of strange alien faces, rectal examinations, flesh excisions: all of TV night-time history was in their minds. Please God! Don't let this be a UFO: maybe a weather balloon, a sun dog, two big K-Mart pillows in the sky, a Salvador Dali hologram.

But wouldn't you know it. Ten minutes later, the twin GIANT GLOWING ORBS REAPPEAR, right above the horizon line. Now it's getting really serious. And it's the worst thing imaginable. You're out driving in the middle of a goddam desert, emptiness everywhere, no other traffic on the road, Yuma is somewhere over to the West, but that's small comfort because its always been a notorious prison town for Westerns.

There's no one around, just this rent-a-car with three jack-rabbit frightened passengers, like a little mechanical desert rodent slinking through the sagebrush and the sand, watched ominously by those GIANT GLOWING ORBS in the sky. And there's no movement: no fade in or fade out, no 90 degree sharp zooming jump-curves in the sky like in **Sightings**, just GIANT GLOWING ORBS tracking the car, probably waiting for their main chance to do another of those famous body snatchings. Who knows, maybe the rent-a-car has accidentally drifted into a previously unknown patch of the Bermuda Triangle, this time flipped right out of the Atlantic ocean and like a rippling time-warp wave motion coming to rest on a little triangular zone of the Arizona parched desert-land. All the conspiracy theories are exhausted now, all the chat is finished, words turn to dust in your mouth at the unwanted chance to be the next alien victim of the day on **Unsolved Mysteries** and even Crash is starting to get on everyone's nerves: it's a suddenly eerie monstrous desert out there, like a huge vacuum cleaner for petrified human flesh, and the desert (human) rats trapped in car scooting across the sagebrush are plenty scared.

The video suddenly ends as nowhere, just like it began. Everyone looks at Joe, and he just says: "It disappeared again after half-an-hour or so. After that, I did a lot of reading and talking to people in Arizona about UFO's. Everyone in the desert's got a sighting story."

Extremely anti-climactic. We were promised a genuine UFO abduction story, and what do we get: flickering images in the sky at high-velocity through a car window, and a narrator who has disappointingly survived without even a trace of an alien probe. But Joe is disappointed too. He tells us that resident UFO media types in Phoenix asked him immediately if he had stopped the car and recorded the sound pattern usually associated with all the passing-UFOs. When Joe says no, they just shrug their shoulders and tell him that the media will never buy his story. He's got to get the rhetoric of the image-simulacrum down for the next visitation by those GIANT GLOWING ORBS. The media demands UFOs like collectibles: like the first issue of the Barbie doll or the 1954 Mickey Mouse watch, the media wants its authorized UFO sightings to fit a certain rhetoric. Those stationary, idling GIANT GLOWING ORBS just won't cut it with the media astronomers.

(To prove the point,) David, our Montreal UFO animator, has been watching it all, but he's dead-skeptical. Standing up, he looks Joe straight in the eye, and like a truth-in-TV-alien-sightings Texas Marshall, he drawls: "I really **believe** in UFO's, and I really **want** to be abucted someday. But these things just don't look right, something's suspicious. UFO's don't stay still, they're not stupid moons, they move around the sky at hyper-velocity. Those disks are kind of alien-challenged: they just hang out in the desert sky."

The TV screen goes cold blue in the middle of the room like an electronic campfire, and favorite sighting stories begin to drift from cyber-mouth to virtual ears. Skepticism's the digital order of the day mixed with just a bit of apprehension and, certainly on David's part, deep longing for the coming of the Alien Messiah. At another time, at another biblical place, and with another sect, we'd probably be sitting in caves around the shores of the Dead Sea with stories wonderful of the coming of the Messiah, with sightings glorious of the Savior, but it's 1995, we've just been probed by a travelling Hi-8 with its images mysterious of those GIANT GLOWING ORBS in the night-time Arizona desert sky, and we'll have to settle for waiting for the millennium, waiting for the Aliens, waiting for our own hoped for disappearance into those GIANT GLOWING ORBS.

EBOLA VIRUS

We recently received the following email from New Orleans:

> It's interesting that an Ebola outbreak has become headline news at the same time as it is publicized in a national bestseller (**Hot Zone**), feature film (**Outbreak**) and TV movie-of-the-week (Robin Cook's **Virus**).
>
> Nick Marinello

Interesting all right. Third World viruses for First World profit.

The Ebola virus is the first of all the media-assisted diseases. Providing just the right metonymic touch of veracity for the "real" outbreak of the Ebola virus in the internal organs of the mediascape, the Ebola outbreak was diffused by a media system in desperate need of a truth-referent to prop up the sagging mass of hysterical (media) reports about body invasion by viral infections. Not only fear of viral infection by alien contaminants in novels, films, and TV movies-of-the-week, but hysterical anxieties about the invasion of the American social body by alien viruses on all the network news, **Prime Time** scoops, **Night Line** and particularly all the talk shows.

But if the Ebola outbreak could so quickly become a viral star for the day, it was probably because there was no outbreak at all, only a bunker culture that has long ago successfully immunized itself from alien invasion. Not a Hot Zone, we're actually living in a cold zone, immunized from uncontrollable outbreaks and certainly innoculated against strange viruses. In this case, the Ebola virus is a perfect **virtual** disease, a right-wing disease – an ideological support in the form of panic viruses that plays subliminally on fear of the breakdown of the immunity system of the social. The media appearance of **Outbreak**, **Hot Zone**, **Virus**, and the Ebola Virus are perfect supports, then, for the will to (viral) purity. Less interesting in themselves, the virtualization of the Ebola outbreak says a lot about the political conditions that gave rise to their popularity and acceptance.

The bunker state mentality always requires a dangerous outsider for its sustenance. What could be better than the Ebola virus with its barely hidden traces of a more ancient fear of African immigrants coming to infect the West? Just because the panic fear of the spread of the Ebola virus is so (medically) far-fetched, it's perfectly (media) reasonable: it supports, in the end, the will to bunker down and blockade the whole continent, and all this with a strong feeling of moral righteousness.

The media is getting ready for millennial frenzy. It projects the Middle Ages onto the end of the century. The Ebola virus is perfect. Like the "establishing shot" in cinema, the Ebola virus is the "establishing disease." It anchors down all the media frenzy about our disappearance into an infectious mediascape.

TIME FOR A TUMS

NEWSWEEK Cover Story: "Teen Violence: Wild in the Streets"

The cover shot is straight from the Vietnam era: smudged imagery of an anonymous gunman stalking traffic in the streets, with a high-velocity rifle in his hands. Teenager as urban terrorist. Not really an aberration from American culture, but its celebration. The inside header provides the correct rhetorical clue: "As every sergeant knows, nothing is more dangerous than a 17-year old with a gun." And then, "the body count is rising...virtual epidemic... violence... is becoming a way of life."

This might be, but the ad on the back cover for Toyota Acura hasn't got the message. Or maybe it has. It's an ad photo displaying a Star Trek version of the Acura beamed down under a freeway loop, highly aestheticized, totally isolated, with a High-Definition purple sky, perfect for a cyber-twilight. The ad copy pitches digital being.

> The Acura Legend Coupe LS was designed with a very specific driver in mind: one who believes if you're totally isolated from the driving experience, it really isn't a driving experience.

There is no driver in the isolated "driving experience" of the ad photo: it's a "legend" fit for travel only in the cyber-twilight. But no matter, the virtual aim is clear: to "make you feel less like an adversary of the road than an extension of it." As for the crowd? "With a 230-horsepower, 24-volume V-6 engine, it's not something you're likely to have to worry about very often."

Flipping back to the front cover with its sinister image of teens with guns, I realize that Acura knows something about "Wild in the Streets." It's offering us an armored personnel (consumer) carrier as a bullet-proof way out of the "virtual epidemic" of violence. Acura is a predator machine: its driver-function hard-wired into the road.

The Toyota Acura ad on the back cover sings us a corporate lullaby: Technology is our friend. "I love what you do for me." It's all a perfect rhetoric of digital culture: the threatening social (that's the 17-year olds with guns); the escape technology (that's Acura speed where the social vanishes in the rear-view mirror and you actually become the road); and, finally, the cynical thanksgiving prayer for our technological salvation ("I love what you do for me").

This is fast abuse, crash society and slick cars, and the telematic self needs a hospice.

If you look inside the front cover of **Newsweek**, the self is delivered straight from urban stress into the hospital by way of a quick self-test for stress. The accompanying ad may be about heartburn, but it's really a fast probe of your virtual flesh. This is no longer about cars or human beings, but the fate of cyber-bodies on a virtual road trip.

The test goes like this. Do you experience these symptoms?
1. Frequent heartburn attacks
2. Frequent use of antacids
3. Heartburn waking me up at night
4. An acid or bitter taste in my mouth
5. Burning sensation in my chest
6. Difficulty swallowing

I think of the Acura driver fast-fused to the road as its body extension, and wonder if it has brought its Acura flesh to the virtual hospital recently. There's an epidemic of violence, and I love what you do for me.

Time for a TUMS.

HACKING THE XEROX ALPHABET

During a tour of Xerox Parc in Palo Alto, California, I am introduced to the inventor of Xerox's entry into the magic realist contest for a new cyber-alphabet for the third millennium. In actual workplace use, Notepad computers involve heads-up scanning (restaurant orders, taking warehouse inventories) and require easy character recognition of data entries for their just-to-the-minute use. The old twenty-six letter alphabet with its problems of character recognition and messy scribbling (that all the optical scanners in the cyber-world can't read) just won't cut the digital grade. Not to worry. The young Xerox hacker, intense and digitally exuberant, perfectly befitting the founder of the **Virtual** Gutenberg Galaxy, had just invented a new easy to use and even easier to learn graphics-based alphabet for Notepad culture.

Our tour guide enthusiastically chirped in that ten minutes is all it takes to master the new cyber-symbols. A quick learning curve for post-alphabet society. Stunned by this missionary display of technological hubris, I remembered the fate of the Japanese written language when it was discovered that all the characters in the Japanese vocabularly couldn't be made to fit the computer keyboard. The solution was obvious: dump half the characters of the Japanese language and go for a leaner, meaner, digitally powered up Japan. Probably noticing my slight hesitation before I bent my knee to the rising sun of the Virtual Word, the Xerox hacker said: "Hey, if you don't like this alphabet, come back this afternoon. I'm almost finished a second virtual alphabet."

SHOPPING AMERICA

Warren Padula

PINHOLING THE MALL

Warren Padula

Warren Padula's photography captures the soul of shopping. Using a pinhole camera of his own making attached to a shopping cart, Padula works in the tradition of covert photography. Forbidden to take photos in the mall, covert photography sets in motion a strategy of counter-surveillance. Not high-tech surveillance cameras idly scanning shoppers as they wheel carts through the lanes of the mall, but covert photography as a way by which shoppers can actually look back, capturing in photographic images the secrets of consumption that the mall never wanted photographed, and certainly not discussed.

Secrets? Like supposedly inanimate objects that suddenly come alive on the shelves, mutate into living creatures if only for an instant, are startled by the quiet presence of the pinhole camera, and just as suddenly drop back into their steady-state pose of dead merchandise. Think, for example, of those figurines that look like an eerie precursor of the coming union of Michael Jackson and Elvis Presley. Perhaps a warning in advance from all the shelves of all the malls that the 90s would wind up waiting for the Messiah: Elvis Jackson. Or consider the young child in the shopping cart that by a strange double motion mutates into a little bunny. In fact, maybe it is a bunny in the mall conceived as a new peaceable kingdom for animals. See the two faces in the photographs? The one of the guy with the American flag tattooed on the sleeve of his jacket and the other of a woman's face: exhausted, emptied out, just flatlined. In both images, their energy is sucked away by the big consuming machine of the mall. A kind of white noise flesh under the neon lights that produces faces you sometimes see at 4:00 A.M. on a hot summer night in the Albany bus station, waiting for a ride to Tallahassee, Florida.

Padula's covert photography captures so well the delirious world of shopping objects come alive and the emptying out of the self as flesh is propped up into a waiting pose for one last purchase. The pinhole camera actually sees beyond the space of the mall to the repressed folds of time hidden within. A third eye, the pinhole camera captures in lavish, but grisly, panoramic views the architecture of the mall as a site of disembodied heads, decontextualized objects, and deterritoralized desires. Pure confusion!

From an early age, we have been trained in the policed optics of the consumer eye: always look at objects directly, only see one item at a time, separate objects from their setting. The consumer brain works to filter out the delirium of the mall. It functions to impose on the mall a false sense of concreteness, a hallucinatory sense of the real: mistaking objects on the shelves for the objectless, floating character of the space. But the pinhole camera is different. Rejecting the repressed eye, it refuses to forget. It is always mnemonic. Behind the false reality of this delirious world of objects, it captures the ghostly presence of absences: plays of light and shading that abruptly cut the blast of hyper-fluorescent lighting, camera views that take us by surprise because they come from below, cutting the empty space of the mall with long-exposure time. Possessing only two "control" features—the length of exposure (measured by the removal of the lens cap) and the type of film used—the pinhole camera breaks forever with the traditional optics of the camera lucida and camera obscura, introducing instead a great rupture in perspectival vision. As Padula explains:

> The history runs from the Camera Obscura (a dark room) which used a pinhole and projected onto the wall to Camera Lucida (a portable prism for tracing), then to photography which was a chemical way to freeze the image which was already there but had to be traced. The return to the pinhole ruptures the perspectival vision of the *lens*, mostly by forcing an extreme close up and attendant distortion that Galileo and others designed out of their lenses.

The pinhole camera can evoke so well the dream-like, or nightmarish, quality of the mall because it blurs the edges of perspective, narrowing the camera's eye to a dark and hallucinatory tunnel vision. Against the totalitarianism of ordinary cameras that impose a "surgical vision where things are always cut off outside the frame," the pinhole camera darkens and narrows perspective as if to return the missing and ambiguous qualities of depth and absence to the camera's gaze. The filtering of lights and images of the mall through the eye of the pinhole camera serves as a filter by which the repressed language of time passing, of intimations of melancholy, are forced back into visual experience. With the pinhole camera, the metaphor of the sheer white fluorescent light of the vacant mall architecture is cut by the metonymy of the *ironic eye*. And if the pinhole camera functions by the technique of long-exposures "to turn people into ghosts" and things into delirious hallucinations, it is because Padula refuses "sharpness" of photographic detail in favor of being "interested in big images." What we lose in surgical optical quality, we gain in acquiring once more a sense of the full horizon of mall experience: its ghostly presences, trompe-l'oeil toys, excessive implements, and winking figurines. The pinhole camera refuses the topos of framing and the minuteness of detail, all the better to draw out the inner, hidden codes of the shopping experience.

And it's perfect. Shift the framing moment of the camera from the standup posture of the adult shopper to that of a child in a shopping cart, and the mall suddenly becomes surreal. The eye of the child, the eye of the pinhole camera, strapped to the shopping cart. Both see the objects for what they are—larger than life, stacked to the ceiling, and vaguely menacing in their inertness. Objects ready to come alive, and people ready to mutate into their phantom other. Here the aesthetic imagination of Max Ernst flips out of its painterly productions, and mainlines the spectacle of the mall. Toilet seats, bananas and stacked cans of Pepsi take on the look of hyperreal bricolage: menacing, filled with repressed fear, ready to topple over onto our heads. Vegetables metamorphose into sinister ruins, like weird biological specimens of yet to be discovered life forms bubbling up from under the ocean's floor. And perhaps not even a world of objects, but body prosthetics for cosmetic care of the kingdom of suburbia: lawnmowers, rakes, wheel-barrows.

The pinhole camera is a different way of looking.* And that different way of looking reveals one of the truths of shopping. It's the Inferno as a site of ecstasy and exhaustion. A slack-jawed, dead-eyed time in the vacant space of abundance.

---

* Warren Padula's pinhole photography is found throughout the book.

SHOPPING THE GAP WITH NIETZSCHE

"I've got a game I like to play. I like to see how far I can get into the GAP before a salesclerk says: 'Hi! How are ya'?'"

Alexis

Leif Harmsen

Nietzsche wears khakis?
You bet!
A pre-GAP kind of guy
who wrote **On the Genealogy of Morals**
for an age when philosophy couldn't be haikued into
regular, slim or relaxed fit.
When people hadn't yet learned
how to recline
by shopping at the GAP

circulating among all the black and beige
and navy and white
But then, the GAP is post-Nietzsche
Because it's about the post-human body
like a hole, or a space in-between, where the body
goes to disappear by fitting in,
just vanishing into frenzied inertia:
that's styles in memory of events that never happened,
or into a neutral-zone: the GAP is **not** the Abyss
it's a recombinant store where the basics
can be folded, spliced, and resequenced
And why?
Because the GAP manufactures our fantasies
"That shirt would be **terrific** for golf!"
"These pants are nice for now,
but **great** for Bermuda this winter!"
"Everybody should have a flesh-colored bra in their
wardrobe."

a nowhere style of clothes
which are never really in,
yet never really out
no cuts, no transgressions, no disturbances, no gaps
without Nietzsche digging in the soul-meat
without conscience-vivisectioning for relaxed fit minds
without body-vivisectioning for slim fit morality
without nutcrackers of the soul for regular fit looks
Where the post-human body in the mall
happily disappears into **The Genealogy of GAP.**

SHOPPING THE INFOMERCIAL HIGHWAY

All night
I zap the infomercial superhighway
Stop the Insanity
Aerosol Hair for Balding Guys
JoJo's Psychic Alliance
Cyber-Spaghetti Makers
Better Memory Talk Shows
An empire of delirious signs
for virtual shopping
where objects float away from the world

Warren Padula

balloon upwards like fat, fluffy clouds
across the video horizon
taking my dreams with them
And I'm totally hooked:
testimonials for mops
with gospel-meeting fervor,
screaming hosts
who just convince me that I can't
live without this all-purpose automatic anal prober
and body spray
Just right for alien abduction,
And I know
that I truly can't
Because it's not the objects
I want
but the hint of uselessness
that they flaunt so seductively
and which they conceal
so beautifully
in the din of the big-top video circus hard sell

SHOPPING FOR TIME

In future shopping, time is all. And so, the paradox: the longer the human life span, the less time there is to actually live. We have never had enough time to go around, and have been compelled to rush our lives in a kind of lingering time depression zone. Always too many obligations to meet, too much mental gridlock, and never enough (Euclidean) time to get through the day. But trode into virtual time, and the problem is solved.

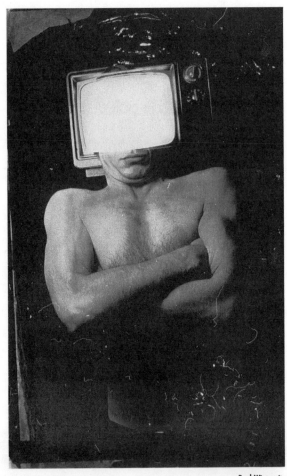

Paul Winternitz

Future shopping for the body electronic is about network-ing for time: time compressed, speed time, recombinant time, memory time, "what if it were?" nostalgia time. No one has to be satisfied any longer with the finite time of the body organic, now everyone can shop around for artificial time vectors. Off-the-shelf virtual time available for just one electronic debt pulse on the forehead scanned.

Time compressed is great! Why not take all those memories with their fantastic, but no less necessary, waste of storage space, double-click them into mega-gigabyte sized time-compression files, and put them away for a better time. Virtual memories always available for instant data retrieval, always mixable with events present and future, and always perfectable by just the right digital dose of happier memory algorithms.

And it just makes good (shopping) sense too. Doctors have found that as we age short-term memory is the first to go, forcing us to recall the same stock-footage of ancient, long-term memories. So, for the body organic, a happier aging process can be prepared in advance by practicising happy memory repetitions for the long term. For the body cybernetic, virtual memory solves the problem of short-term memory loss by warehousing in our neuro-circuits only a carefully edited file of our life. It's better that way: time-compressed for a life decompressed.

Just got an e-mail message. My external 850 meg. HD will be ready next Tuesday. Can't wait!

SHOPPING THE SECRET
VICTORIA'S SECRET

Deep red velvet curtains with gold tassels, Roman
striped wallpaper, low rose-colored lights, and a mirror
that always lies.

Red satin, pink lace, black lycra, Maidenform bras,
thong bikini underwear, silk pajamas, a softly diffused
smell of sachet.

What is Victoria's secret? Maybe it is the dressing-room,
the mirror, the essence of sachet?

Victoria's Secret can be your secret
Cellulite fades away in the dark
Small breasts can be enhanced by the Wonderbra
The stomach can be flattened by a lycra slip
Midriff bulge can be masked by a long-line bra
Or don't think about your body's flaws and slip into a
diaphanous negligee
Victoria's Secret can be your secret
with its dressing-room wonderful
as a dense sign of the body imaginary
Where you disappear into the mirror in the soft light
becoming all sorts of people,
playing back dreams of intimacy
Victoria's Secret can be your secret
In front of the mirror you always look your best

Posing head up high
stomach in, back straight
dreaming ahead to a lover's touch
remembering a glance from a lover's eyes
Victoria's Secret can be your secret

This can all be your secret
Until you exit the dressing-room
into the mall with its fluorescent lights
and the mood of your body deflates
from Victoria's Secret
with its deep red velvet curtains with gold tassels,
Roman striped wallpaper, low rose-colored lights
and a mirror that always lies
back into the body flawed
that stands exposed to the mirror of life.

BAUDRILLARD AT THE *EXPRESS*

Certificate of Authenticity

> Created of soft knitted fabrics that emulate those perfected in France generations ago, Express Tricot captures the most desirable qualities of fine knit clothing. Tricot has always been favored by Parisian designers for its fluidity of movement, smoothness of shape and, above all, great fit. Modern French women appreciate its resilience and versatility and regard it as the ideal expression of chic, relaxed fit.

The Ecstasy of Communication? Words so sweet they just pop off the page, mingle with the clothes, and almost allow you to smell springtime in Paris on the racks of Express designer-wear knockoffs for the body resignified.

Written in both French and English, the certificate of authenticity comes from a red mohair sweater that I bought recently at Express; actually on the same day that Jean Baudrillard, the famous French theorist of simulation, was coming to dinner. Now I knew Baudrillard was keen on visiting American tourist sites that had been recycled into second- and third order simulacra, from Disney World to Universal Studios, so I suggested a quick road trip to Express. What could be better: a Dayton, Ohio clothing company that had mutated into the all-American sign of French chic, and a French cultural philosopher whose writings mirror **America**.

The architects who designed Express must have read Baudrillard in advance because it's a perfect sign-system: more French than France, more stylish than Catherine Deneuve. It's where French fashion disappears into that which it always wanted to be: American design. And why not? Express is **the political economy of the sign:** the perfect fusion of good old American know-how with the French counterfeit. French acoustic pop music played softly in the background, neo-classical columns, a lot of marble, and racks and racks of great looking clothes: long pinstriped jackets with velvet trim, flowing crepe dresses with tiny flowers that would be perfect for your summer holiday in Aix-en-Provence, and a hand-knit sweater that looks like it belongs on the shoulders of a French student on her way to the Sorbonne (probably to study American fashion and business English).

What is the **fatal attraction** of Express? Why the obsession in America with the iconic sign of French fashion? It doesn't matter what the original site of production (Hong Kong, Thailand, China), what counts is the Parisian sign-value that's breathed into the American clothing. And there's some heavy breathing at Express: Parisian chic and French design, a whole fashion **simulation** of boul. St-Germaine, but only better. These aren't Parisian prices nor are they Parisian clothes, which makes them all the more sought after by American shoppers. Look at those fabulous images of **seduction** that line the walls – French models with berets, scarfs, simple white T-shirts, or knitted sweaters that you really do believe come from Paris. The "counterfeit" that Baudrillard loves to talk about actually has its sign-value lifted off the streets of Paris, landing with a fashion thud in the malls of America. So, for some **cool memories** of those sentimental late evening walks along the Seine or that café espress that you once shared with a friend at the top of the Beaubourg (the one overlooking the entire city of Paris, from the Sacre Coeur to the Eiffel Tower with Pere Lachaise and its **illusions of** [Jim Morrison's] **end** always lingering close by) you don't have to travel to the Left Bank, just drive to the mall and take a warm fashion bath in all the **simulacra** of Express.

Just like Baudrillard who shops the **fatal strategies** of Express Tricot, and finally chooses a white T-shirt (with an Express Tricot tag on the outside, but a "Made in America" label on the inside) for a Parisian friend. He goes to the cash, and says to the salesclerk: "Bonjour"

She panics, gives him a startled look, and blurts out: "What? I'm sorry I don't understand French."

Baudrillard looks baffled for a moment, shrugs his shoulders, and then turns to me and says: "Oublier Express."

THE LEMON YELLOW COAT

I didn't need a lemon yellow coat. Who does?

Even when the price is just $29.95. Even when **Glamour** magazine declares the new fashion line: "Color is more than an accent... let black play backup." And I thought to myself, Yes! I'll give it a try. What a great idea: black as backup.

So I hurry back to the store to check out **my** lemon yellow coat. It really was my coat even before I bought it. Once I've finally decided to buy anything, the trip back to the store is always like a dreamscape. Lemon yellow coat with black leggings? Lemon yellow coat with a long black dress? Velvet? Wool knit?

Wait! What's going on here? Someone is trying on my lemon yellow coat. She says, "I've got to have this coat. I need this coat."

I listen and watch. Glad that she likes it because I had a queasy feeling that the coat might be a bit too garish. Of course, I know she's going to buy it, and now I want it even more than before.

She tries on the coat. It has no buttons, no closings at all. She turns to her friend and sighs: "I can't buy this coat. A coat needs buttons. There are no buttons." She puts the lemon yellow coat down and leaves the store.

I try the coat on again. Who needs buttons? It's a $29.95 lemon yellow coat straight out of the pages of **Glamour** magazine.

"Highlight your body's strongest feature," exclaimed the fashion spread. A coat, a lemon yellow coat? What be my strongest feature wrapped in lemon yellow?

SILVER LADY ON QVC

candles on the table
and light reflected in your eyes
833 sold
3 minutes and twenty-three seconds to go

Warren Padula

TALKING DAYTIME TV

Mama's got a hangover
and Daddy's lost his spleen
Daughters hate their Mothers
and their Mothers want to scream

Margo stabbed her husband
and Sid shot his wife
Tammy slept with Daddy
and Daddy smirked "All right!"

Suzy likes to party
and Jamie drowned the kids
Mary-Jo is a hermaphrodite
and so confesses Liz

Of soaps and cereals
and buns of steel,
of singles and swingers
and therapists who heal

Of smiles and sleeze
and guys on bended knees
of TV jokes
and just plain folks
with broken hopes

and vile men
and terrified women
and a TV crowd that
stomps, boos and cheers
but nobody really hears

Now they say that Oprah's wise
and Richard Bey despised

Shirley's like the rest
certainly not the best,

Ricki's held up high
with glamor in her eye

Dohahue's asleep
with Geraldo in a heap

And Jenny Jones?
well they're just calling her a creep

we're talking TV
we're talking Daytime TV
we're talking you and me
Can't you see
We're finally free
to sit down
and watch
more TV

DOORS OF MISPERCEPTION

Hacking the Future is the cultural politics of the 1990s. It's about decoding the present and recoding the future: breaking into the ruling algorithms of contemporary politics and society, and creating new cultural algorithms for the virtual future.

TWO BLASTS

Everybody who lives in the late 20th century is a potential hacker of the future. And why not? Everything has already been blown to (digital) bits by the power of virtuality. Life at the end of the second millennium is about living in the aftermath of a violent implosion of culture, politics, and society. In the short space of a single century, human experience has suffered a double technological blow. First, it has been fast-processed by the invisible media of electronic technology. What McLuhan could only prophetically talk about in the 50s and 60s is already an electronic reality that is in our past. Just when we understand the grim implications of McLuhan's warning that the invisible media of electronic communication have outered the central nervous system, that is, when McLuhan really does make common (electronic) sense, technology does a quick flip, and we suddenly find ourselves living at the end of technology (in the form of an external mediascape) and at the primal beginning of the age of virtual reality. And this is the blast that hurts. Because now it's no longer the central nervous system that is being externalized or ablated, but technology gets a life, detaches itself from the human species, and begins to grow a new telematic body just in time for the 21st century. Two blasts, then: one *electronic* (that has ejected the nervous system from the privacy of the body), and the other *virtual* (that has rubbed together the externalized central nervous system with the soft language of algorithmic codes and began to grow a new "distributive species": distributive intelligence, distributive sex, distributive feelings, and distributive sight). After this double implosion, life as we know it is like one of those immense stellar meltdowns where we're in a spacecraft riding at the edge of the known universe, experiencing all the while the shock-waves and spatial perturbations of this violent decompression of society and seeing all around us the zooming debris of the human wreckage.

Ironically, the privileged media of electronic technology provide us with perfect viewing-screens on the virtualization of human flesh. TV is a great portal on cultural implosion: a just-to-the-minute visual simulator of how (our) bodies are virtualized by gigantic image-based processors, freely resampled, and then played back to us for humiliated applause. Music is a favorite listening port for our disappearance into cyber-ears. Cinema has now been reconfigured into special effects to give us the actual feel of human flesh as it is coded into blurs of sight and sound and image-matrices, and then speed-forwarded into digital life. Think of *Forrest Gump*, *Braveheart*, *Apollo 13*, and *Waterworld*: monuments to the disappearance of cinema into special effects.

The media of the electronic age are the future museums of the body virtual.

FLESH LAG

We live now in a time of flesh lag: that moment when the human body as we have known it is in the process of being replaced by digital organisms—data skin, algorithmic minds, cyber-vision, soft nervous tissue. While it is always sad to say goodbye to one soon-to-be-extinct (human) species, we can always take (cyber) heart because we're also present at the creation of our digital successors. And not just saying hello, but getting up to speed and going hyperflesh with the best. That's hacking the future. Refusing nostalgia for the death of being human, it puts the body on fast-forward, trying to outrace the future of the digital body which, in any case, is just beginning to crack its way out of its cyber-egg.

There are a lot of hackers of the future around who might look on the outside like they are stuck in old-fashioned human bodies, but if you practice just a little misperception, just a little trompe-l'oeil, and catch them hyper-thinking when no one is looking, you'll see a hologramic shift sweep over their flesh as their senses suddenly go on-line in digital high-gear. Most electronic artists are like this: they have 20th century bodies, but 21st century hyperbolic minds. The will to be more than virtual, to become human again by becoming more than digital, as they hardwire themselves to the future virtual. True interzone bodies, electronic artists are involuntarily, and certainly for better and for worse, geographers of a new territory: living at the interstice of two species types—human and android—floating in a folded space of anamorphic perspective and alien eyes and algorithmic skin, trying to pretend that everything is normal, that they're not the earliest star voyagers to a bodily planet that already exists in screenal consciousness, even if their physical bodies are just too slow, and will always be too slow, to catch up.

Test riders on the virtual storm.

BODY HACKING

The computer has already begun hacking the 3rd millennium: actually hacking the human species, virtualizing human experience in a matrix of cyber-codes, rendering flesh, creating terminal communities, and installing in the human sensorium Operating Systems for emergent (electronic) senses. Whether we like it or not, the choice now lies between hacking the future or being hacked by a computer world driven by the will to download the human species, flesh and all, into data storage files for better management.

Hacking the future is our historical destiny in an age in which digital reality is the deepest language of contemporary culture and society. We live now in a wormhole called digital reality: the primal beginnings of the co-penetration of flesh, mind, and data. Not human reality as surplus flesh or digital reality as surplus virtuality, but the genealogy of something really new being born: data flesh, chip minds, hypertext philosophy, nano-art, cyber-sex. The digital sky darkens at its opening dawn, only to better reveal the emergent senses of data flesh as its most brilliant morning star. For the good and for the bad, for the disappearance of being human and the appearance of being digital, for cyborg mutants and outlaw rendering machines, we slipstream our way into hacking the future.

HACKING FLESH

Interfacing

That's hacking flesh. The will to virtuality is a war machine directed against the singularities of nature and social nature. It harvests the body for digital reality by a biological tactic: break down the immunity systems of flesh, and clip the weakening organ with a viral implant. The infection takes hold, the forcefield of digital reality overrides the fatigued organs of the human species. This medical procedure of implanting cyber-sickness inside the human organism is what, in computer language, is called interfacing. A low tech example of this is television, which weakens the body's immunity system by presenting itself as only entertainment, puts the brain on sleep-function, and then quickly reconfigures the human sensorium as the 7-second brain. The 7-second brain? That's TV producer talk for the new digital cycle of audience attention-span.

Rendering

That's hacking the brain. Distributive intelligence for a fully distributive culture. No longer brain flesh buried alive inside the coffin of the skull, but the cyber-brain taking a ride on the Internet, and then saying what the hell, and going full-out multi-media on the World Wide Web. A neuro-product of modelling, rendering, and mapping, the cyber-brain rips itself free from its connection to the spinal cord, hard-drives consciousness into a single cybernetic code, and gets down to what has always been the most ancient business of cybernetics: the language of the helmsman; the language of control. Not the mass mind, but the virtual mind will be the ruling intelligence of the 21st century.

Cloning

That's hacking the human species. Just as in the 1950s people in the United States were used as unwitting sites for radiation and germ warfare experiments, in the 1990s radical experiments are underway in bio-tech labs to clone the DNA of the human body, to mix species types, to grow simu-skin, and to create laboratory organs. This is all accomplished under the guise of improving the human condition. The cultural implications of the Internet pale in comparison to tissue engineering. For example, American scientists were recently on the verge of replicating a new species type by mixing animal and human

DNA. When ordered by the Government to cease their eugenic experiments, they refused, stating that this was "too important" a medical breakthrough. Designers of a new species type, eugenic scientists are the agents by which recombinant organs will be created.

HYPERTEXT MINDS

Hacking the Future continues McLuhan's concept of artists as probes—with this key difference. For McLuhan, artists were early radar systems for detecting major transformations in technology, probes that went ahead of the general population much like the earlier tradition of the artistic avant-garde. *Hacking the Future* is about going faster, deeper, and with greater intensity into the interface between being digital and being human. Privileging human "wetware" rather than hardware or software, *Hacking the Future* is about creating cuts, disturbances, and transgressions, like a space or an interzone, between digital reality and human subjectivity. Certainly not a theory of "understanding media," *Hacking the Future* begins with the assumption that traditional media have been superceded by hypertext flesh, 7-second brains, and wetware minds. Human beings always go faster than technology because people have always been hypertext: fully linked, netted, downloaded, parallel processed, and interfaced. Virtual flesh is always ahead of technology, and that's the terrain explored by *Hacking the Future*. Thinking ourselves as wetware to the hardware of technology and the software of the coding labs finally opens our minds to the doors of misperception.

HACKING THE FUTURE

FOUR EXITS

Exiting Nietzsche: The 20th century might have begun with Nietzsche's prophecy of the death of God, and the triumph of the will to power, but it surely ends with the death of the human species as we have known it, and the disappearance of the will to power into its opposite—the will to virtuality. The will to virtuality? That's the powering down of human flesh into the society of what technotopians like to call "virtual incorporations". The computer coding languages of interfacing, rendering, mapping, and modelling provide the first predatory signs of an emergent life-form—the fusion of digital reality and recombinant genetics to produce a *virtual* species. That the contemporary century ends with epochal breakthroughs in tissue engineering, artificial intelligence, and recombinant genetics as preps to the creation of artificial flesh indicates that today all tech hype is a coverup for *our* terminal future.

Exiting Marx: 20th century politics has taken place under the sign of Marx's historical understanding of the triumph of capitalism: the explosion outwards of the commodity-form, the ascendancy of the bourgeoisie, and the seeming eclipse everywhere of the labor movement. But if the fall of the Berlin Wall signals the end of 20th century politics and the beginning of 3rd millennium history, then 21st century politics will be marked by the swift emergence of the digital commodity-form in the historical disguise of pan-capitalism, which strutting alone on the stage of human history and without its traditional historical check of socialism, is at last free to *be* its dark homicidal double: fascism. In the 1990s, the fascism that was supposed to have disappeared with the military defeat of *National Socialism* in the 1940s appears everywhere in the form of retro-fascism, feeding on the same political psychological diet of national humiliation and economic depression: LePen's 15% of the French national vote; ultra-right, ultra-white (but certainly not ultra-bright), armed militia groups in 47 American states; extreme right-wing movements in Russia, Austria, Germany, France, Italy, Belgium, and Canada. No longer the spectre of Communism, but now the hard reality of the "will to purity"—pure bodies, pure politics, pure ethnicities, pure hatred. Far from being exceptional, the genocide of Bosnian Muslims is a symptomatic sign of a resurgent right-wing "global village."

Exiting McLuhan: In the 60s, McLuhan theorised that the technological media of communication were in his term, "extensions of man", electronic outerings of the central nervous system. But that was then, and this is now. Because in the 90s it's exactly the opposite.

Not technology as an extension of the human sensorium, but the human species as a hotwired extension of digital reality. No longer the will to technology, but the vanishing of technology into the will to virtuality. Hacking human flesh by way of artificial intelligence, virtual reality processors, and the violent force-field of the electronic media is the sure and certain way by which virtuality actually eats the human body, becoming digital flesh at the end of the century.

Exiting the 20th Century: Beyond Nietzsche, Marx, and McLuhan, *Hacking the Future* is pulp theory. That's pulp for the end of the millennium, when all the bodies are piled up one mile high. Not virtual or heavenly bodies, but bodies that are trying to cope with life lived in the twilight hours of the 20th century.

A schizoid culture that divides sharply now between the technological dynamo of the will to virtuality and its attendant virtual class on the one hand, and a spreading detritus of human remainder that can't be absorbed by digital reality on the other: surplus bodies, surplus labor, surplus nations, surplus flesh.

Two tendencies then: the will to virtuality from above, and the vicious ressentiment of conservative fundamentalism from below, with human remainder stuck in-between.

Pulp theory is the story of human remainder told through the medium of 90s culture. It's our thesis that the language of digital reality has now fled the high tech labs of Silicon Valley, MIT's Media Lab, and the cyber-grids running from Tokyo to Grenoble and Munich, taking up residence in the violent force-fields of everyday cultural experience: shopping the GAP, visiting Las Vegas, Daytime TV, Arcade Cowboys and Suicide Drive, or the transgressive aesthetics of "Slash and Burn" as young bodies in California try to "feel" in a culture that is numbed and purified.

MILLENNIAL POLITICS

Retro-Techno: The Politics of Fear

The political tendency today is to the right.

The 90s began with a decisive split between two opposing political tendencies: the triumphant technotopia of the virtual class, and diverse forms of retro-fascism. Like a rapidly mutating cellular mass, this split was of an extremely short duration, lasting only four years from start to finish before it evolved into something very different. Under the impact of a *managed* worldwide economic depression (that drove working- and middle class adherents of welfare state liberalism towards right-wing populism), and the failure of the so-called "information superhighway" to live up to its utopian billing (that drove members of the technological class into the waiting game of bunker individualism—the psychological breeding ground of conservative fundamentalism), these two previously divided, and bitterly opposed, movements suddenly merged. Their combination in the ideological form of retro-techno, which is to say the merger of the fiscally conservative, morally puritanical, and anti-government populist energies of the right with the technocratic know-how of the virtual class, this merger of reactionary politics and techno-knowledge, produces the dominant ideology of the 90s. An example of this is a recently convened conference entitled "The Aspen Summit: Cyberspace and the American Dream II" where, as *The New York Times* reported, conservative venture capitalists, self-proclaimed former hippies and anarchists, and "cyberspace prophets" came together to discuss the role of government, law, and communication in the "knowledge society" of electronic networking. It was perfectly retro-techno, beyond the traditional labels of Republican and Democrat or conservative or liberal. Marc Porat, chairman of a Silicon Valley software company, was quoted as saying:

> The people here are from the center of politics, from the right wing, left wing, apolitical, technology and the arts, and what they're seeing is deep changes in culture driven by deep changes in technology... People who hold deep political prejudices have to set them aside.
>
> Peter H. Lewis,
The New York Times, Aug.23, 1995

Of course, what Porat doesn't say is that the proceedings (organized by the "Progress and Freedom Foundation") are being hardwired directly to Newt Gingrich as backup material in developing America's new (neo-conservative) telecommunication policy, and that the silent consensus position of all the participants seems to be that no government is the best government, particularly when it concerns political regulation of the rising technological class.

Until now, the political right has always been the default position of society: the tendency that doesn't produce social change but acts reactively in clawing back its manifestations; which doesn't create new visions of political history, but acts retrospectively in seeking to return to an earlier, supposedly more innocent, time. The appearance of retro-techno as 90s dominant ideology changes this fundamentally. Today, the political right is actually authoring the Operating System of society.

The ascendancy of retro-techno cannot be described in the old dialectical terms of class struggle. The upsurge of right-wing ideology in the 90s is more like the Mississippi flood, a vast swollen river fed by powerful tributaries, flowing inexorably towards the sea, cresting in city after city along its way, breaking the dikes, and leaving a big clean-up job in its wake. Retro-techno is like that: a vast, roaring political river fed by powerful political tributaries—right-wing techno-libertarianism, Ayn Rand style; the moral right with its obsessions against gun control, abortion, and pay equity; populist fiscal conservatism with its special pleading for tax cuts and contempt for the welfare state; and corporate austerity programs with their eye only on the jobless economy. Flooding country after country, cresting here, receding there, taking everything in its path: Chirac in France, Gingrich and Dole in the United States, Major in Britain, Harris, Klein, and Finance Minister Paul Martin in Canada. When retro joins techno, the political horizon of life in the 90s is finally coded in. However, the nostalgia for innocence by the political right is very selective. *Time* magazine stated recently that the US "debt" would disappear almost overnight if corporate taxes returned to 1950s levels.

Deadly innocence for the total eclipse of the brain.

Sex Without Secretions

Arthur Kroker, Marilouise Kroker, David Kristian, Steve Gibson

S pas M
VIRTUAL REALITY, ANDROID MUSIC, ELECTRIC FLESH

Book/CD
ARTHUR KROKER
Music by electronic composer Steve Gibson
Introduced by Bruce Sterling

*Written from the perspectives of cultural politics, music, photography,
cinema and cybermachine art, SPASM explores the ecstasy and fade-out of wired culture.*

"A postmodern prophet — may be the Marshall McLuhan for the 1990's." — *BBC.*

"Mixing wit, bombast, and parody, Kroker's work stands alone." — *Mondo 2000.*

"In purely compositional terms there are some really wonderful juxtapositions, liquid mergers, and dimensional effects." — Jacki Apple, *High Performance.*

"SPASM is an explosive mixture of cyberpunk and social critique... a remake of Videodrome, navigating in the territory of the new digital frontier." — Roberto Aita, *la Repubblica.*

Published in the USA by St. Martin's Press — ISBN 0 312-09681-X.
Published in Canada by NWP. Distributed in Canada by McClelland & Stewart — ISBN 0 920393-35-7.

DATA TRASH
the theory of the virtual class

ARTHUR KROKER & MICHAEL A. WEINSTEIN

DATA TRASH explores our obsession with cyber-culture, and our fascination with the disappearance of the human body in virtual reality.

"... when the shadows grow deeper, and skeletal hands pull the curtains closed, and the talking heads of CNN glow like gibbous moons in the corner, and the majordomo throws another Branch Davidian on the fire, then my choice is clear: I'll pull my collar up and hunker down under the rusty springs of the couch with a heaping helping of DATA TRASH" — Bruce Sterling, *Mondo 2000.*

"On the post-cyberpunk techno-theory circuit, the name of the future to watch is Arthur Kroker." — *The Observer*, London.

Published in the USA by St. Martin's Press — ISBN 0 312-12211-X.
Published in Canada by NWP. Distributed in Canada by McClelland & Stewart — ISBN 0 920393-23-3.